RICHARD EVANS

THE TALENT
MAGNET

Employer Branding and Recruitment Marketing
Strategies to Attract Millennial Talent

Published by WriterMotive
www.writermotive.com

To all my friends and family who help through the bumpy road of life and business.

Forever grateful.

CONTENTS

PART 1
THE SITUATION

INTRODUCTION

It's predicted that, by the year 2025, more than 75% of the global workforce will be made up of Millennial talent.

Some call them Gen Y; others label them Millennials. Whatever you wish to call this generation, it's true to say that those born between the early 1980s and the late 1990s think differently, act differently, and ultimately react differently to any other age group. They have different ambitions and views on work to those that came before them.

The workplace has grown used to the traits and characteristics of the baby boomers. They have ruled the roost for a long time, and organisations have adapted to their needs and behaviours. So much has been said and written about this cohort of society that has had such a large impact on just about every aspect of life. But as the baby boomer generation heads towards retirement, employers are being forced to think about who will replace them. Let's not forget: the baby boomers were brought up after the war in a world that had yet to see colour television, let alone the internet, mobile technology, social media and cloud innovation!

As Millennials have entered the work arena, much has been said about their ability to fit into the existing workplace. They have been characterised as lazy, entitled and even narcissistic. This stere-

11

otype seems to have stuck! But, being children of the information age, Millennials bring different skills to the table; they know how to use technology better to find solutions and to get ahead. This means that they can produce work efficiently. Since when has being able to identify the fastest route to a solution been classified as lazy? There almost seems to be a vested interest from those in positions of power in keeping out these ambitious newcomers, but the Millennials are not all that the negative press has made them out to be.

Alongside bringing a different skill set into the workplace to that of those that went before them, they bring a different mindset too. And getting employers to adapt to the needs of this generation has been a major issue. It is important for employers to embrace change to attract the best talent to grow their company. In order to do this, they must understand the needs of this generation and know what they consider as important.

Also, as an organisation's customer base changes, they need like-minded individuals to grow the business towards that new customer base. And over the next 10 to 20 years, who will dominate that new customer base? Millennials, of course.

Employers, as a whole, have had to start to adapt their talent attraction strategies and techniques to appeal to whatever workforce they want on their books. Consideration for many different factors has to be made.

The fact that university education has become more accessible over the last 30 years means that Millennials are generally well educated. They are well grounded in technology because they grew up around it and make use of it in their daily lives, thus increasing their ability to carry out more than one task at a time. They hunt in packs and find that they can bounce ideas off each other to create solutions for workplace problems. (This is a very different approach to the lone-wolf worker that is typical of the baby boomer cohort.)

For Millennials, there's an emphasis on finding a balance between life at work and precious time spent outside it, so flexible working conditions and the ability to work from home are paramount. They feel they should make a meaningful contribution to society and that their work should make lives better for people.

Even the structure of a company may have to change in order to keep its top Millennial employees engaged. This generation thrives on feedback; they want to know how they are doing and how to get ahead. This puts pressure on the management structure to engage talent in new ways. Employers need to promote a set of working practices that will appeal to their team. If not, their team will up sticks and move to a competitor that better suits them.

The ability to come up with creative solutions within an existing framework is another aspect of work life important to the Millennial. For too long, big employers have wanted to constrain their employees with structure, lines of reporting and rules of conduct. The type of company that appeals to Millennials has a much looser structure that encourages collaboration between different departments and the use of different techniques to solve the problems that they face.

Millennials are looking for an employer who will mirror their own ambitions. The ability to progress quickly by hard work and problem-solving is an important asset in an employer. An employer that is socially and environmentally responsible is also highly valued, because the Millennial wants to be seen to be doing positive work. For employers who want to attract and retain the best talent for their company for their future prosperity, the landscape is shifting dramatically.

But none of this is going to be easy. And it can't happen overnight. It will be a bedding-in process where the employers of today gradually evolve their company and employer brand into the employer of the near future. I say the near future, because the Millennials are already out there. They are already in the workforce, in big business, in their own businesses, and they are looking to the future. As the influence of the baby boomer generation starts to fade, a new force is emerging. Millennials are starting to influence and dictate the way that they want to work, the way that they want to be managed, to be motivated and to be influenced themselves. The winning employers are those who are aware of this phenomenon and who are putting plans in place to make the most of it. The losing employers are those who expect every new generation to fit into (and be attracted to) the old way of working.

This book will help you become a winning employer of choice.

21ST CENTURY
TALENT ATTRACTION

The information age has well and truly taken hold. Every aspect of life is displayed for all to see online. The internet is a huge source of information and the wiki model means that information is constantly updated and refined. If someone offers inaccurate or unhelpful advice on the internet, it is quickly superseded by better information.

Business is no different to any other aspect of modern life when it comes to the internet and the information age. The climate has changed for business in so many ways over the last 20 years, the last 10 years, the last 5 years and even over the last year. The fact is that it is constantly improving every single day and will continue to do so. Technology has become a catalyst for change, as some industries have leveraged technological advances to go digital, disappearing from the physical world entirely. Others have fought and fought the advance of technology, and find themselves now at a crossroads.

Take the estate agency industry, for example. Traditional high street estate agents have dabbled in technology through property portals, and most have an internet presence through a cursory website, but the industry is really quite resistant to the change that technology brings. There is currently a wave of online-only estate agents that are in direct competition with the high street agent. The high street agent sees these new firms as cowboys who don't understand the game. To them, they are simply a nuisance. But the game has changed and industries don't look like they used to. Those that aren't reacting are getting left behind, and those that are taking advantage of the changing landscape are forging completely new versions of industries that have been around for centuries.

The world's new reliance on technology can be a double-edged sword. The consumer's buying dynamic has changed: often a customer interested in buying a product has done 60–70% of their research before a salesperson gets involved. This is exactly what is happening in the job market too – so when it comes to recruiting and retaining the best talent, you need to get this right.

In the past, it was your job advert, your job specification and your communication with applicants that defined the perception of the job role. There was a narrow definition of what the job entailed, which was completely controlled by your own job description. From there, you were able to control what people thought of the job that was being advertised, and to convince the applicant that it was what you wanted them to think it was.

Back then, young would-be recruits were told by careers advisers to have a look at a company's website if it was possible, to find out what they did, what they looked like and how they operated. People would sometimes write to a company to ask them what they did and get a glossy brochure explaining the structure of the company and how the employees fitted into this structure. Employees were always valued, always a part of the big picture and always painted as well-rewarded.

Nowadays, if the truth is somewhat different to that, your potential new recruits will know about it. The average candidate can use the shortcuts that the internet provides to get straight to the details that they want to see. They can find out instantly if they believe your company fits what they are looking for. The Millennial candidate doesn't mess around applying for roles with companies that don't match their high ambitions. A Millennial will be able to cut to the chase, and decide in a very short period of time whether they want to apply or not. If they do, you will see the applications flood in. If not, you may never see or hear from them. Because modern life is so connected, your internet presence can lose you potential applicants as well as gain them for you. This is how critical it is to get this right.

The changing business landscape and the connectivity of the internet have a huge impact on attracting the top Millennial talent. Your company profile is there for everyone to see. It is a straightforward process to look on your Twitter feed, your Facebook timeline or your website, or to find your current employees online to see what you are all about. Your job advert may say that you are a progressive company that gives recruits a great opportunity to progress quickly if they display the right talents and behaviours. But if the current team do not agree with that you may find comments on social media that suggest that it isn't the case. If your company website and careers site shows a different level of professionalism or a changed set of values to your job specification, your potential recruits will be able to sniff this out and you will lose applicants that once you were able to attract.

Richard Evans

With the changes in communication that the information age has brought about, the cat is out of the bag. Your company *becomes* what the public perception of it is, not what you want people to think you are. With just a few clicks of your keyboard you can find more information than you can ever process about almost any company in the world. Who founded it, how it was founded, customer reviews, news articles, complaints, trading figures, recent job losses – it's almost always out there somewhere. Your potential applicants will know all about you before they make that application, and may or may not follow through their interest based on the information they find.

Big business tries to fight this with their own information. Most large companies have their own blogs on their websites that deliver positive information about the great things they do. They have multiple press releases every month and employ marketing companies to publicise their positive work and reduce the impact of anything negative. Information can counter information. If you find a newsfeed full of stories about how they look after their team, you are far more likely to apply than if you read about a round of lay-offs that happened only a few months ago.

Of course, the information age started with the PC and rapidly progressed from there. To be able to sit at a desk and find out information about anything on the planet was liberating for many people and a goldmine for businesses. A company found that it could now sell its products to more people in their own country or open up new markets in other parts of the world. When the PC became really personal through the use of mobile technology, tablets and smartphones, this moved to a whole new level. Now your company profile can be looked at by someone who is sat in a coffee shop, on their sofa at home or travelling on the bus to work. You can never escape or ignore your internet footprint. Once something appears on the internet it is often there for life, so it is part of the rich tapestry that defines your company and what you are seen to be. A good profile can make the difference between success and failure when it comes to recruitment.

Do you value your team?

Is there a real scope for progression?

Is the bonus any good? Is it achievable?

Is the company financially sound?

These are all questions that potential employees want the answers to, and they are better positioned now to find out this information than at any time in the past, because of the information age.

Information is swapped freely because it helps others and because the information is free, it is valued. This may seem a little strange, so let me explain. If the provider of the information is giving out data for no reason other than to share it with the world then it is more likely to have been provided with good intentions. If someone is paid to give a view, a conflict of interests may occur and the payment may alter the accuracy of the information. The internet bases a lot of assumptions on the fact that people are inherently good and the information they provide is designed to make things better. Of course, this cannot apply to every single piece of information online, but the fact is that there is so much information that the parts that are uploaded with malicious intent will be heavily outweighed by the truth. This is called aggregating and the effect is that the truth will come out because the misleading information will become a smaller and smaller proportion of the sum of information as time goes by.

You are seen everywhere, in everything you do, and recruiting top talent will be no different to this. Most companies have social media profiles, company websites, are mentioned in the news, on forums and chat rooms plus many other areas of the internet. LinkedIn is a great networking tool for business, and can lead to making great relationships to partner other businesses or to get more work done. But you will have a presence here and many of your team will as well. This means that it is easy and fast for a potential employee to contact members of your existing team to do some digging or ask questions about the company. Some of your team may not reply, but if there are team members out there that feel there is vital information that a potential employee should know then this information will pass hands from the existing employee to the potential one. It can have a positive effect, if the existing team member is feeling valued and rewarded, but it can also have a negative one, if they feel that they have been mislead or under-valued. Your existing employees are a great asset in managing and distributing information about your company because they are having the real-life experiences that will be almost identical to those of your next recruit, and the one after that.

The information age is constantly reshaping the market that business operates in. The advent of information as an asset that directly affects what goes on your profit and loss is quite a new one for business to get to grips with, but it is happening all around us.

When it comes to advertising a new vacancy, the information about you directly affects the talent pool that you will be fishing in.

Get it right and you can be looking at better applicants that will take your company forward. Get it wrong and you could end up treading water, or worse. A better quality of applicants will save costs – you need advertise your vacancy only once, because you will get the applicants you want the first time. It will save time because you will be able to select from the first list that hits your desk. You can avoid a vacancy sitting idle in your company for several months because you can't find anyone to fill it.

So we have seen in this chapter that you cannot hide your online presence and internet past. Employer branding across all digital platforms is becoming more and more important in candidate-driven markets. Candidates are now in control, and they need to be 100% sold on the hiring company before taking the first step. If they're not, you'll get a smaller pool of applicants, and a smaller pool of applicants will inevitably mean that you get a smaller choice and more than likely a lower standard of new recruit.

The information that the world holds about you is accessible 24 hours a day, 7 days a week and 365 days of the year. So the trick is to make sure that you are able to turn it to your advantage.

MILLENNIAL TRAITS AND DESIRES

Let's take a look at the Millennial character traits and what attracts them to potential employers, before we move on to look at how to build a strong employer brand identity and how to implement intelligent recruitment marketing strategies to attract the best talent.

'The 12 Hallmarks of The Millennials' listed below are formed from my personal experience interviewing over 1500 Millennials looking to embark on pastures new.

There are so many skills that your team of Millennials can bring to the workplace, from their mastery of technology to their teamwork. They are ready to be challenged and work hard to help your company achieve its goals. It is your task to ensure that your company is ready to accommodate them in order to gain everything you can from their skills. It can make the difference between the continued success of your company or potential failure of it. The best companies of the next 10 to 20 years will be those that can embrace and exploit the characteristics of the Millennials to enhance what they offer their customers. To do this, however, you need to attract them to your firm in the first place, and then provide a work environment that is conducive to enhancing their talent.

'The 12 Hallmarks of The Millennials'

1. Millennials are multi-taskers

The ability to truly multitask is one of the great assets of the Millennial. It has come from their upbringing with mobile technology. It enables the Millennial to work on different projects at once. It allows them to stop in the middle of something and come back to it later in the day or in the week. This is a massive positive for any employer, as they can quickly change focus and deliver what is needed within a task or project.

2. Millennials are team-orientated

The Millennial is completely at home in a team. They thrive in the collaborative process and can easily bounce ideas off each other without causing a large degree of friction. This is a great asset for any company as they look to their teams to take more responsibility for their own work. The Millennials in your team will step forward, work as a team and crunch the solutions for you and your customers. They can work like this with minimal supervision and then disband and form another team for an alternative task. Mixed in with the multitasking, this creates a dynamic workforce that can quickly adapt to the situations employers (and their customers) face.

3. Millennials are tech-savvy

Growing up in and around the ever-changing technological advances has brought the Millennials strongest suit into play. They grasp technology in the workplace at a pace that most baby boomers can't manage. They are quick to pick up different systems, different forms of communication (with colleagues and customers) and different ways of solving a problem. This pulls together all the other skills mentioned above. A competence (a real mastery in most cases) of technology enables collaboration, communication and multitasking at a level that those that went before the Millennials often can't achieve. It is amazing how one skill that has come about because of the environment the Millennial grew up in has impacted so many other skills that employers now need to make the most of.

4. Millennials are socially connected

As the first generation that really took hold of social media and text messaging, the Millennials can operate with minimal instruction. They have long been used to reacting to short text, Facebook or Twitter messages that they don't need long-winded instructions to carry out a task. They will often get the gist of what is being said instantly and will ask questions to confirm their understanding. Employers love a team that can react quickly with minimal instruction and disruption. Your typical Millennial will be able to do this in a heartbeat because it is what they have done all their lives. Forward-looking companies have taken social media to their heart and see it as a source of good, not to mention somewhere they can do business quickly and cheaply. The Millennial fits right in here, as they feel completely at home with social media.

5. Millennials are efficient

Millennials know how to use the tools at their disposal to provide solutions that work. They have the ability to manipulate the internet to find the answers they need and are used to producing quick results at school, at college and at university. If you can quickly provide a result by doing online research that draws on the work of others, why not follow this route? Gathering relevant information quickly is a great way of producing results by amalgamating the work of others. It is linked to the collaborative process but doesn't necessarily need to have the collaborators present. Do you allow (reasonable) internet access at work? Can your Millennials get the answers they need from search engines? The Millennial will be more efficient by looking up answers on their smartphone while they are working at their desk. You may run the risk of the internet being used for social media or catching up with the news, but you will also enable your team to produce for you.

6. Millennials are results-orientated

Millennials operate at a level where they want to see the results of their actions. If your company is disjointed, with some parts working in isolation from others, the Millennial might feel that can't see the results of all their hard work. Millennials are results-orientated, so you need to let them see the targets and the achievements of their efforts. Keep in touch with your team and share with them on a regular basis the figures that matter. If one part of your team has worked particularly hard on a certain project then share the results so you keep your Millennials and your whole team focused and motivated for the next project. Feedback is the lifeblood of any working relationship for the Millennial.

7. Millennials want to learn at pace

We've just read that Millennials are proud of the hard work they put into their job and they really want to know what their line manager feels about their contribution. Why? Because they want to learn how they can progress and develop quickly. The feedback process is a large part of this. The skill of the Millennial is to turn it into performance. They desire the knowledge that can help them to reach their goals. The company that wants to attract and retain the best Millennial talent needs to make sure their feedback process is robust. The average Millennial has been raised to have their sights set high and they need the information to be able achieve what they set out to do. As they have their sights set on a bright future, they know that they require some direction and that the best way to see where they are going is to fully understand where they presently are. Your role as employer is to put them in this position and set out a defined career path to get them where they want to be.

8. Millennials want to find meaningful working

The average Millennial wants to find meaningful working to supplement their meaningful life. As a group that has been brought up to understand the wider world in a way that no other group before, the Millennials know that they can make a difference to the lives of others. Meaningful work turns a job into a career. Meaningful work turns and employee into an asset. Meaningful work changes the way that your team view what they do every single day when

The Talent Magnet

they turn up to work. If you can keep the Millennial interested in what they do then they will stay with you for the long-term. If the Millennial also understands and believes that the work they carry out makes a difference in the lives of others then it takes on a meaning that the they will put their heart and soul into. This can be incorporated into your charity fundraising as a business and your CSR programmes.

9. Millennials want instant gratification

But the Millennial isn't all about the long-term. Everything in modern life has become instant. The world that the Millennial has grown up in produces answers straight away. They have never really learned to wait for anything, because they have never had to wait for anything. Millennials want instant gratification. In terms of their employment, they want to start a new job, understand what is required from them, master it, move upwards and then repeat. The Millennial will be able to get to grips with the tasks you set them, especially if technology is involved, and then be ready for the next task. On the way you will need to praise them, show them the results of their actions and encourage them to improve on the process. They want to understand what is going on, be left alone to do it and then be shown the success of the work they have carried out. The answers need to be as immediate as you can make them. If they produce a piece of work for a client today then the Millennial will want to know how it was received tomorrow. It is this level of instant feedback, giving rise to gratification, that makes the Millennial clock tick.

27

10. Millennials want flexibility

The world has moved on from the Monday to Friday, 9 to 5 exist-
ence of the offices of the past. There are so many other pressures on
time that the average Millennial needs to be able to manage their
own time to a certain degree. Millennials want flexibility from their
employer, and if you don't provide it then there will be someone
else that will. Modern life has taken all kinds of twists and turns in
the way of time and time management. You may need your team
to be talking to clients in different time zones or to meet clients in
the evening or at the weekend. Your team members may want to
leave early to see their children's school play or come in late because of a late client meeting the prior evening. There are all kinds
of reasons why a standard day doesn't fit everybody every time. By
allowing a degree of flexibility over timekeeping then you will have
a team that is happy and that will give as well as take. This inspires
your team to go the extra mile and produce high quality work for
you. It inspires them to commit to work projects out of office
working hours. It helps them to understand that you view them as
a human being with a life outside of work rather than just someone
who works for you. Inspire the Millennial and see great results.

11. Millennials want autonomy

Millennials will quickly understand the things that are required of
them and will work out a way to make these happen at the right
times. The ability to prioritise and complete the work in the required timeframes is a skill that the average Millennial has in
abundance. They need autonomy to be able to produce for you
what you want. It is the opposite of having a worker who you need

to constantly look over with every task. If you explain the process properly and give a deadline, the Millennial can be left to come up with the goods with minimal supervision. Add in instant feedback and the opportunity to progress and you have a Millennial who is properly motivated to keep on delivering high quality work time and time again.

12. Millennials want adventure

Millennials are the first generation for whom travel is at the core of their culture. Sabbaticals, gap years, travelling and holidays have left this cohort with two core values that any employer needs to take into account – the fact that the millennial values their lifestyle highly and that the millennial has been exposed to different cultures and values. The Millennials have seen much more of the world and are more aware of what is going on in their own backyard. They want to see this world. Millennials crave adventure. This is as true in their work life as it is in their life away from work. If you offer the Millennial a chance to work in an environment that offers learning new techniques, developing new strategies and the opportunity to go overseas as performance incentives, they will jump at the chance. The way of working that involves rising to a challenge, trying something completely new and adventuring into new skills or areas of work is the perfect job scenario for the Millennial. If you become stable and stale as a company then you may struggle to keep hold of your Millennial talent because they seek out adventure in their work. The worker of the past was fearful of change and struggled to adapt. The Millennial has grown up in a world of constant change as has learned how to cope with it. They see change as an adventure to journey on rather than a foe to battle

with. Keep your team full of top Millennial talent and the changing world won't be something that your company is afraid of. Your
team will embrace it.

You need to understand 'The 12 Hallmarks of The Millennials",
and take them into consideration when developing and communicating your talent attraction strategy and employer brand. This will
help you engage directly with the best talent on the market.

WHY RECRUITING SHOULD BE YOUR #1 PRIORITY

"Hiring is what you do when you let the world know that you're accepting applications from people looking for a job.

Recruiting is the act of finding the very best person for a job and persuading them to stop doing what they're doing and come join you.

Hiring is easy and fast and is basically a retail operation. Recruiting is artful and slow and is essentially a direct marketing effort."

—*Seth Godin*

It is well known now that the biggest factor determining the success of a business is its people. Ensuring that you have the right people in the right positions, and making that a priority, has a direct impact on your bottom line. The only sustainable competitive advantage of a company is the recruitment and retention of the best people; people are a company's greatest asset.

So far in the book we have looked at the Millennial and the importance of attracting them in the information age. We have seen the skills, the behaviours and the needs of this group of employees that have started to move through the workforce. Their number and their influence will grow as time goes on. As they take over from their predecessors as the largest group in society and the workplace, they will dictate to larger society their needs and desires. Recruiting great talent is one of the biggest challenges that a firm will face. There is a war for the best Millennial talent and the competition is fierce. In this chapter we will look at the reasons why recruiting top talent should be your number-one priority if your business is to grow successfully.

It's been found that unfilled vacancies cost the UK economy a staggering £18bn a year. (Indeed.) You need to make sure you are minimising the effect of this lost revenue on your business for a healthy bottom line. As Indeed's Senior Vice President Paul D'Arcy says, 'For today's job seekers these are positive conditions, however, at around £18bn per year, the cost of unfilled roles should serve as a wake-up call to UK businesses developing recruitment strategies in a post-recession environment. Each empty desk represents an opportunity both for the individual and the business. For the business, finding and recruiting the right individual means better productivity and profits, while for the individual, earning an income and spending a salary contributes to wide economic growth. In today's economic environment of lowered unemployment and labour participation, it has never been more important to hire the right fit for each role.'

The average Millennial has no fear of changing jobs, changing employers, changing career or even setting up on their own. Start-ups are big business with the Millennial generation. In days gone by, a job was seen as being for life, and it usually was with only one employer for the whole of your career. You chose the company you worked for when you left school and stayed there until your retirement, when you got a gold watch and a pension. This was no doubt driven by two factors: the organisation looking after its employees, and the employees' fear of change. That fear of change, the fear of the unknown has disappeared from the mindset of the Millennial generation. The Millennial will happily move to another company if they feel that they aren't valued or that the grass is greener elsewhere. Life is seen as an adventure, change is seen as good and it is all about experiences rather than time served.

This freer movement of labour is one of the reasons that more vacancies exist in the job market of today. By the very nature of the job market, there are always unfilled vacancies. It is quite a natural part of the modern recruitment process, and is exacerbated by the notice periods in most work contracts. The lag between one employee resigning and another being ready to take their place can now be several months long. Hiring the wrong person after such a delay is costly to your bottom line and can be fatal to your business. You need a new recruit to be able to hit the ground running and be flexible enough to adapt to whatever your business wants to do next.

Technology is advancing at a faster pace than ever. This is another important factor that influences why hiring Millennial talent should be your number-one priority. You need a robust and flexible workforce that will take your company into the next 20 years and beyond. The business models of the future will need workers of the future. We have already seen that Millennials are adaptable, up-to-date with technology and that they provide solutions to the problems modern business faces. These skills will only ever be in more demand in the future. They will be the ones that take your business forward when others are standing still. Social media – along with the fact that so many businesses have moved (or partly moved) online just extends the fact that you need a team of workers that can rise to these changes and challenges, and propel your company into the next generation. The company that stands still here will fall behind because there is so much activity happening. The Millennial is not afraid of this challenge and you need to get them on board with what you want to achieve as soon as possible.

Finding the best Millennial talent is not about just looking for any employee. You need the right employee. To simply hire the first applicant that walks through the door is doing a disservice to the role. If you have a vacancy, then you want to fill that vacancy with the best talent on the market. Every vacancy is an opportunity to hire the best talent. To have a role for someone and noone to fill that role means you are losing out on income, your customer is potentially losing out on service and the economy is losing out on activity, wealth and taxes. This can be a difficult concept to drill down to the level of just one company, but the overall number of unfilled vacancies in the UK economy is costing billions of pounds in lost revenue.

The next generation of your customer base is Millennial. People like to do business with people like themselves. This means that a business should mirror its customer base. If your customer base is the Millennial, your team should reflect that. You want to be able to move with your market. Modern business dictates that customers need to be constantly engaged in what you are doing; they don't have the same level of brand loyalty that existed in the 1980s and earlier. Nowadays, you can't snare a customer once and expect to keep them for life. You have to work hard to keep them interested and involved. A customer that thinks they are being treated as an individual is far more likely to stay with you.

Pursue top Millennial talent as though your company depends on it – because it does depend on it. If you want to be a competitor in the business world of the next 20 years, you need to think like the biggest companies around. They have irresistible employer brands, talent programmes, graduate programmes and management training programmes because they understand what it means to look for the best talent from the upcoming generation of Millennials.

You need to think carefully about your place in the market you operate in. You need to make sure that you can compete with those around you in terms of offering the Millennial generation a route into your business and through to the top levels. Don't forget their desire to move onwards and upwards. They want to get ahead in whatever work environment they operate in so you need to make sure that you have systems in place to attract and retain them.

Are you happy settling for second best? Or do you want to stay ahead of the game and pitch yourself above your competition? The good news is that you can compete with the big players. But if you want the best, you need to fully commit to the recruitment, attraction and retention process. You need to look at the bigger picture. Take a step back. Put yourself in the shoes of the talent you wish to attract. Would you be champing at the bit to join your team?

This is where it gets interesting. The rest of this book will look in-depth at how to implement employer branding and talent attraction strategies to create a business that Millennials queue up to join.

PART 2
THE PROPOSITION

BUILD AN IRRESISTIBLE EMPLOYER BRAND

As we look at the ways that you, as an employer, can attract the top Millennial talent, it is important to consider all angles. When you send out your recruitment adverts, are you pleased with the response? Do you feel that your vacancy should bring in far more applicants or a far better quality of applicant that it has done? One of the reasons this might happen is known as employer branding. An advertisement looking for employees for firms with a compelling employer brand will often get significantly more responses than one for a local company that doesn't have that level of presence. There are some companies that just have that feel about them.

So, what is employer branding?

We've discussed how employees are your biggest asset; the good ones are hard to attract and even more difficult to keep.

Can you justify why you are a good place to work? Put simply, good employer branding is all about living, breathing and communicating this message in a way that is so compelling that potential employees are queuing up to join your business.

We are talking about perception; how the wider community views your business. It influences the kind of online presence you have, the engagement you have on social media and it's a factor in the number and quality of applicants you get for any vacancy you advertise. Once your brand has a reputation for quality, you will start to see benefits. Your reach grows as your name gets out there. This can be on a global scale like Google or Facebook, or something more niche in the industry you operate in. Recognition brings you access to a larger pool of talent. People will reach out more to you and your company.

So this actually goes to the very core of everything you do as a business. This is about your marketing, the way you treat your employees and the relationship you have with your customers. Being a brand is about setting expectations and then living up to them. It is about leading rather than following and it is about living and breathing everything you do.

Developing your employer brand is not an easy exercise. It takes time and effort to be the very best you can be in your chosen areas. From the outset you need a clear vision. The vision sets out everything you want to be and everything you want to be seen to do. Leaders in global businesses always set goals for their company. HP's current careers website statement is, 'You're driven to make positive changes. We're driven to find people like you. We have a lot in common. Let's change the world.' That is, that meaningful work is at the epicentre of all of their duties. When this ethos oozes out of every pore, they are obviously an attractive company to work for. Their vacancies get a great response from potential applicants because of their employer branding. They have got it right, and the response from the job market is overwhelmingly positive. Each vacancy that is advertised is in demand. They have a larger talent pool from which to select their next recruit, and they continue to rise onwards and upwards with the best talent.

As I have said, this doesn't happen overnight, but you need to be in a position to make it happen for your company, for your brand. So, let's start at the start.

Sit down and take a really good look at your operation. Decide what it is that you are great at, good at and what you can do better at. Remember that recruiting and retaining the top talent is hugely important in today's job market. It is competitive out there; you are fighting with other companies to secure the best people. You need to have a single vision. When you look at your performance in attracting new recruits, don't always assume that the answer is money. Lots of employers fall into the trap of thinking that to get a better quality of applicant, a better salary is the only option. Make sure that you link in your brand and your ethos to your recruitment. Sing about what you do well, what your vision is and where you want your company to go. If it doesn't make the reader a new recruit there and then, it may make them one in another six months. Or it may make them more likely to buy your product or service. It may make them more likely to talk positively about your company, to mention you on social media or to recommend your vacancy to a friend. Your relationship with the reader may not be a totally direct one, but if they buy into your employer branding then you have a brand advocate. This is someone who will help the word-of-mouth marketing that your brand needs to become one that gets better quality applicants time after time.

But of course, a lot of your employer branding develops away from the arena of recruitment. There are two main ways in which your employer branding will bring you results when it comes to looking for that next member of your team – your existing team and your customers.

Your existing team must be on board with your mission statement or vision. If they are kept informed of what you want to achieve, what you have achieved and share the success stories with them, you will be more successful. If you have a team that wants to work for you, believes in what you do and feels part of that, you have another set of brand advocates. This team will talk positively to their friends and family about you as an employer. They will proudly mention that they work for you. They will tell their friends and share with their social media contacts updates about you as an employer, and this includes any vacancies that you have. Already you have a wider pool of talent to choose from, because you have people working for you that are enthusiastic about working for you. You will be surprised how much this rubs off on others around them.

The culture of a company is evident in every piece of marketing, every department and in every employee. The culture determines how the team works, how customers are dealt with and who does what. The culture is obvious to a customer and obvious to a potential new recruit. Remember that with the internet age, every potential new employee can look up huge amounts about your company and what you do. The internet footprint of your company tells a lot about your culture. How many customer complaints are aired, what colleagues say about the business on their social media accounts and any news stories about how the company behaves itself are all part of the wider culture of a company. This is all embedded in the culture of the company and can be difficult to change.

But with the business landscape changing every day, your company needs to change with it. To attract Millennials to your business and persuade them to stay you will have to get your culture right. The way in which you behave towards your employees has to change over the next few years if you want to position yourself as the right destination for any Millennial who is looking to get ahead in their career. The culture change may have to be facilitated at the top but the actual nature of the change will come from the whole team. As the team interacts and starts to develop the way they deal with customer requests and workplace problems, the company needs to roll with that and provide the flexibility of time and resources that enable the Millennial team to produce high quality work. This culture change will help you to retain the top Millennial talent because they will feel as though they are understood and appreciated.

The same goes for customers. If a customer enjoys dealing with you, their enthusiasm for your business will be evident in what they do. They will follow you on social media, interact with your website and keep an eye on the job vacancies you have.

To me, there is a line that can be drawn with employer branding. Just about every company I know sits on one side of the line or the other. On one side are companies that have to seek new recruits; on the other side are companies where new recruits seek them. The job pages of firms with impressive employer brands are just that. They post jobs on their own website, at minimal cost, and wait for the quality applications to flood in. Potential employees will check the site regularly or ask to be notified of any vacancies. The cost and effort that these well-branded organisations have to put in is low. The companies on the other side of the line have to fight harder for each applicant. They have to place adverts, put their vacancies on external websites or pay recruitment agencies to find them suitable applicants. Their spend goes up, but the quality of their applicants doesn't follow a similar arc to that of expenditure. It is more work, more time and more money. It is often the case that these companies put in more to get less at the end.

There are many ways in which you should be developing and communicating your employer brand, most of which will ultimately be covered in the latter chapters of this book. We have seen the impact that a good employer brand can make and I would suspect that the vast majority of employers could see the benefit in this. So the next steps are to make this happen in an effective way that means your recruitment gets easier and attracts a better quality of applicant. It won't take 20 years to build your employer brand but it will take some time and energy to get it right. The act of recruiting gives you the opportunity to have conversations with the job marketplace and to see what they think about your company. The results you get from recruitment give you a good idea of how your efforts are received.

How you are seen in the employer marketplace is affected by how you interact with that marketplace. One way is to enhance your reputation for quality recruitment, quality training and quality supervision. You will need to live and breathe these values with your existing team as well as all of your new recruits to develop this reputation over the long term. Too many companies ignore reputation because it can't be directly measured and doesn't fit easily into traditional Key Performance Indicators. But reputation affects a whole range of areas related to your business. It brings in business that generates income. It attracts web traffic naturally that can turn into enquirers and new customers. Most importantly it gives you a presence with potential employees.

For an employer there are, of course, certain additions to your normal working practices that can really help here. There are accreditations for employers that show they care about their employees. You can go for an 'Investor In People' status or attempt to become one of the 'Top 100 Employers': these awards show your existing team and your potential future team that you care. These awards and accreditations mean that you have looked at your work practices, you have established a level of care for your team and you will continue to do so. As with many aspects of business, there is not one single thing that will transform what you do overnight, but there are a series of initiatives that you can carry out that together will change what you do. If you become a workplace that is known for excellence when it comes to your team then vacancies will fill more quickly with better quality applicants in the future.

It's not just when your team gains a member that you need to think about your employer branding. When your team loses a member then there is work to do too. Understanding the reason for a team member leaving is a great way to make sure that you develop and protect your employer brand. There may be underlying reasons that could cause an issue with other team members in the future, or for the direct replacement for the person who is leaving. You have a duty of care to understand what is happening in your workplace and put actions in place to ensure that any potential problems are resolved. This is all a part of having a great employer brand. It isn't just the team members that remain that you need to take care of. The departing team member could be one of two things to your brand – a brand advocate that brings you more positive energy, or someone who has bad things to say about you. Never let people leave on bad terms if you can help it and be as positive as you can about their contribution while they have been at your company. If you are starting to develop all of the other initiatives we have discussed in this chapter, you will probably find your staff turnover is much lower anyway. But when it does happen, make sure that the leaver feels appreciated and they will speak positively about your company, enhancing your brand.

Your brand will not look after itself. You will have to make sure that you are living the values that you set out for yourself and you need to shout about it to your tribe in your talent attraction process. Once you understand everything you want your company, your brand and your employer brand to be, you must be confident that you are achieving this. You can't have a short-term blast and then sit back and assume it's taken care of. The very best brands live and breathe their values every single day through every single employee and every single action that they take. When you interact with a great brand you are very aware of it; all of the team members add to that feeling that you are in the right place. You need to get your team to this level and ensure that your employer brand and your company brand are well aligned and doing the same thing. Don't forget that today's customer could be tomorrow's applicant and your next new recruit.

EMPLOYER BRAND VS. CUSTOMER BRAND

The values that a customer holds will often be very different to the values that a potential employee holds. The journey and experience is different. You will have a plan to take your new recruits through a period of embedding, training and development that you just can't replicate with a customer, whose journey takes them from customer to loyal customer and then brand advocate. These journeys are not completely removed from each other but are dissimilar enough that they have to be looked at in a different way.

If you simply hold your customer brand up to the employment market, you will fail in many ways. Everything you do when you recruit is judged by the potential employee that you are trying to attract. What's in it for them? You need to speak their language and appeal to their needs as an employee. Your careers website itself is the first step towards you attracting quality employees to your organisation. This should be written entirely with the potential employee in mind. Remember the traits and desires of the Millennial worker.

Of course you can't completely detach the thought process involved in talking to your customers from the one involved in talking to your current and future employees. Often a customer will become one of your employees. This will happen in part because they know of your brand and want to work for the company attached to that brand. You will not retain your team if the employer brand offers a completely different experience to that of the customer brand. Your team knows what it's like to be a customer of your company so you want them to be able to translate that to being an employee. The messages are the somewhat similar because what you stand for is the same. If your company ethos is about making people feel good, this goes for both sides if the equation – your customers and your team. It would be exceptionally difficult for your team to make your customers feel good if they didn't feel that way themselves!

A strong employer brand is vital to your recruitment efforts because it gets your name and your vacancies into spheres that they just wouldn't reach otherwise. This connects with some of the things we have looked at in previous chapters, such as appealing to the strengths of the Millennial worker and getting your name known, especially in your own industry. Your brand reaches potential employees on social media, through networking groups and generates more clicks when advertising online. The brand can work for you when you are not in the office. A strong, positive brand brings customers to your door whom you didn't directly reach out to. It brings referrals and new business from sources that you probably weren't even aware of.

A business's brands for the employee and the customer may share the same values. From the core values of the company and the mission statements produced from them, the key concept is communication. Once a value has been decided as the driving factor behind a company, the next job is to communicate this effectively to the two groups. This forms a large part of the branding exercise. The way in which the value is relayed depends on the audience. Both the customer and the future employee want to know that their interests are being looked after. The alignment of the employer and customer brands ensures that the end goal is one and the same: the company needs both parties to be happy in order to succeed. But for the employee to understand the business and function within it, and for the customer to buy in and spend money with the company, they need different instructions and communication. The strategy is the same, but the method for achieving that strategy is different for each group because the target audience is different.

The synergy between your customer brand and your employer brand will really drive you forward when it comes to attracting and retaining the top Millennial talent. The image that you project will be the one that people interact with. If you have more engagement on social media for example, you have more chance of filling that vacancy with the right person. If you have a large reach on LinkedIn, you will have people asking *you* about potentially job opportunities, rather than the other way round. If you have customers that love your products or services, they will jump at the chance to work for you when the chance arises. Think about how your brand makes you appear, both in the world of customers and in the world of potential employees, because it will make your life easier when looking for talent. But ultimately, remember that both brands have a different job to do and have a different target audience.

PRACTICAL STEPS TO BUILDING A REMARKABLE EMPLOYER BRAND IDENTITY

An employer brand is intangible. An employer brand identity however, is a tangible asset that adds value to your business and promotes what you stand for across all media platforms. A strong customer brand identity commands a higher value premium price. A strong employer brand identity commands top-level talent, the cream of the crop that thrusts your business in the direction you are looking to head.

Step 1: Be clear about what a great employer brand identity can do for your business

Firstly, you need to be clear about what a strong employer brand identity can do for your business.

You will need a budget and some further internal and external resources to achieve this, so the first thing you need to do is get the go-ahead from the decision makers in the company. If you get the best resources available to achieve this, the path to a strong employer brand identity will be a much smoother and more efficient one, and your business will be able to take advantage of the benefits sooner. What are those benefits?

Attract top talent to your company

When the right people are aware of your employer brand identity, you have a group of people that are more likely to apply for relevant roles with you in the future. When you impress people with your employer brand, you have ready-made candidates for your future roles. You have a better quality of applicant to choose from because you have created a brand within your industry that draws talent towards you.

Retain the best talent in your company

The impact that your employer brand has is not just on your potential new recruits. The people that already work for you are an even bigger consideration. If you don't look after them and make them feel a part of your brand, you may lose them to a rival. A great employer brand motivates your team. A great employer brand improves productivity. A great employer brand keeps your best people with you.

Differentiate yourself from the competition

If you want to attract the best talent then you need to look like the employer that the best talent wants to work for. Talent attraction has become more and more competitive and only the best employer brands will consistently attract and retain the best talent. You need your message to resonate with the right individuals and by having an employer brand that sets you apart from the competition then you are well on the road to achieving this.

Increase your profits and decrease your recruitment spend

Creating an employer brand identity does not come for free: it takes work. But in the long run it is a crucial investment of your money that will offer an exponential return on investment. As you gather a pool of talent that wants to hear from you via email subscriptions, social media or your careers website, you will see your recruitment costs fall significantly. You want to attract talent that takes your company to the next level, instead of just replacing what you have. Because of this, creating a strong and visible employer brand identity within your own industry can help you to unearth top performers that will improve your business and subsequently increase your bottom line.

Step 2: Where are you now?

Gain clarity about how your employer brand identity is viewed in the marketplace today, internally and externally.

Before you begin the journey to developing your employer brand identity for the future you need to understand where you are today. This means you have to take an honest look at where you stand to see the areas that need to change.

This includes:

- What is your current team's view of you as an employer?
- What does the job market think of you?
- What are your rivals doing better than you?
- What are you doing better than your rivals?
- How can you improve your recruitment process for all parties?
- What behaviours define your relationship with your employees and future candidates?
- What behaviours do you want to define your relationship with your candidates?
- Does your employer strategy match your overall company strategy?
- What does your current team think are the factors that will attract new candidates?
- How do you market your employer brand identity currently?
- Who are the future recruits are you looking to attract?
- What are the character traits and desires of your target market?
- How do you intend to market to your potential recruits in the future?

The answers to all of these questions will give you the starting point to develop your employer brand identity into what you want it to be.

To understand where you are now, it's a good idea to complete the following:

- SWOT analysis of all factors
- Internal interviews
- External interviews
- Market research into your target talent market

Simply put, you need to know where you are so you can establish where you want to be.

Step 3: Where do you want to be?

To assess where you want to be, it's critical to develop your **Employee Value Proposition**. Your EVP is a clear statement of what you can offer your current employees and future talent. This needs to be completely orientated around the needs of the talent you are looking to attract, retain and engage. It should be a vision of what you can offer right now and what you strive to achieve for the future.

When the EVP is complete, you need to create your '**Employer Brand Bible**'. You want all internal and external stakeholders involved the company to be able to understand and use the employer brand identity to the best effect. This is where your Employer Brand Bible holds its value. It should be a resource for anyone to use to understand the employer brand and how to use it on whatever channel they require. This both promotes and protects the brand, and ensures consistency of message when attracting the best talent. Your Employer Brand Bible will communicate your messages and the style in which you showcase them. This will outline your vision, your core values, your business personality and the manner in which your business operates.

Your '**Employer Brand Bible**' should include:

- An overview of your vision, key values, your tone of voice and your business personality.
- Your well defined, compelling EVP.
- All visual identities, including logos, taglines and the style of communication from a design point of view.
- Your colour palette – this should include all primary and secondary colours that will be associated with your Employer Brand Identity to create consistency.
- Typography style – outline all of the font families that will be used across all media platforms to, again, create consistency in your identity.
- Photography/images & video style – include example of the style of images that represent the style of your brand identity.

If you put the time and effort in at this stage, your Employer Brand Bible will create a template and outline for developing your identity across all platforms at the next stage.

Once you know what you want to achieve, you need to communicate it to the rest of your company. Pull together all the changes you are proposing and deliver them effectively to your existing team. This can be done verbally or by written communication, but it is important because it clarifies the vision you have for current and future employees.It is from this shared vision of the company that you will be able to talk to those outside of your organisation about what you stand for and what you do well.

Step 4: Bringing the identity to life across all platforms, communications and touch points

The design of your brand identity brings it to life and increases engagement. The brand strategy ensures that you are seen and heard in the right places.

When you complete your research, it's time to bring your employer brand identity to life. It needs to sing and shout about all of the things that you want people to know; it needs appeal to the right target group, it needs to deliver the right message and show off what you stand for.

Brand has long been associated with the logo of a company, but it is about far more than that. The biggest brands in the world are now easily identified by their logo alone, but it didn't happen overnight. It took time and investment to get them to where they are today. A brand identity is about the way you interact with your potential applicants and existing employees. A brand is about the feeling you give people when they look to apply to work for your company; the feeling of what it's like to actually work within the business. So this stage is not about putting together a logo and thinking that it will do all of the work for you. The building of your employer brand identity is about everything you do to differentiate, engage and promote.

This includes the design and development of all touch points including:

- Visual identities
- Careers website
- Bespoke photography
- Bespoke videos
- Social intranet
- Mobile app
- Design of social media channels
- A defined social media strategy
- A defined content marketing strategy
- Marketing collateral including adverts, brochures and banners
- Online tests and gamification of the recruitment process

KEY FACTORS TO CONSIDER

The channels on which you advertise your employer brand are designed for you to attract talented individuals to your organisation. Make sure that you tell people what you stand for, how great you are at certain things and what you want to be. This is not about a hard sell, but it is about letting people know what your company is and where it aspires to be. You need to become influential in your industry and this happens by communicating your passion to your audience across all platforms.

Your team is full of individual people with their own lives and stories to tell. These stories can have a massive impact on your ability to attract their peers. The emotion of a real story has far more impact than any promise that you make. Ensure that the stories of your existing team can provide inspiration to your potential candidates.

With the fast flow of information on the internet and social media your reputation can travel much faster than you can fix it, if there are any issues. Make sure that you deliver what you tell people you will deliver. A disgruntled employee can do damage to the reputation of your company in a very short space of time. The brand experience needs to live up to the brand expectations you have created.

Your followers will want to see what it is like to work for you. You need to let them see what the culture is like, what the prospects are and how people currently feel about working for you. The more accurate a picture you can paint then the better fit the potential applicant will be because they already have a good idea of what it is like to work for you. It is also important here to make sure that you add new content, to keep it fresh and up to date.

Your company will no doubt look for recruits in a diverse set of job roles at different times. This means that you will have to appeal to everyone from, say, executives through to shop-floor workers on vastly different salaries with a different outlook on their career. Your messages need to reach all areas of your business and appeal to all backgrounds of employee, with slightly tailored messages that are all consistent with the overriding employer brand message.

Within this stage you will develop all of the media in the various channels you want to use and run them past various stakeholders for feedback and improvement. Throughout this, you must con-

sider how consistent this employer brand is with your customer brand. You will need to keep the lines of communication open and keep the level of support as high as possible. You have worked hard up to this point to gain buy-in from all parts of the company so it is a good idea to keep this going. Once you have a proposition that you are happy with, it is time to start getting ready to launch your identity across all media platforms.

Step 5: Igniting and launching your employer brand identity across all platforms

Here comes the fun part: the launch! Remember, this is a huge marketing opportunity so it pays to ensure that this is planned to perfection to execute the biggest return of initial benefits. Launch the identity internally first to ensure you are all 'singing from the same hymn sheet', and take any initial feedback before it goes public.

Revisit your key objectives before rushing into a launch. Think about what you are looking to achieve and how you are going to do this.

Factors to consider for the launch of your employer brand identity:

- Timing is key: seize an opportunity and create a buzz
- Leverage social networks to engage with videos
- Presenting at an internal conference is a great way to engage current employees and get them on board
- Presenting at a careers fair is a good way to engage to a targeted audience externally

- Create engaging press releases aimed at your target audience
- Promote your brand through brand ambassadors internally and externally
- Communicate what it means to the bigger picture of the company's vision
- Create marketing campaigns to promote the launch including direct email, print and online adverts
- Promote your EVP and Key Values
- Tell your story

Step 6: Monitor, develop and grow your employer brand identity

Although you will no doubt be planning to implement an employer brand identity that you are proud of there is always room for improvement. Feedback is the key to making things better and anyone who has had contact with your employer brand is a valued provider of this feedback. Keep the lines of communication open and be prepared to act on the opinion of your target market.

Your existing team can really help here. When you inspire your existing team to great things this will rub off on the people that they are connected to. Family, friends and social media contacts will be among the first to hear if someone is working for a great employer. This is an extension of your great employer brand because their contacts could be your next applicants. You can encourage this by offering an incentive to your team if they refer someone to your company that goes on to be recruited. This increases shared responsibility and makes advocates out of your current workforce.

Use and promote your employer brand wherever you can. You have taken time, money and resources to produce it, so use it wherever you can. Make sure that your recruitment marketing promotes and reflects the strong brand you have created and this will give it maximum effectiveness.

Keep monitoring what you are doing. The development of your employer brand identity is important every day, not just the day it was implemented. You need to understand the impact it is having and the benefits that it brings and this can only be achieved by monitoring what is going on.

You need to see what is happening in the company and how this has changed from where you were at the start of this process. Ask these questions to gather this data:

- Are applicant numbers increasing?
- Is the time to recruit a new starter decreasing?
- Are internal referrals increasing?
- What do new recruits think after being with the company for a while?
- Do hiring managers see a better quality of applicant?
- Why are people leaving your business and what would have made them stay?
- Is there a lower level of absence in the business?
- Are your team performing better?

By pulling together all these factors, you can form an idea of what improvements your employer brand is making and where it still needs to impact. The bottom line figures of how much is being spent on recruitment will be a major focus at the top of the organisation, but you can apply more qualitative measures such as the fact that better-quality employees will take the company further in the long run. By knowing the impact your employer brand is making on the business you can see where you need to change it and where you need to further its reach.

It is imperative that your employer brand enhances the way in which your company is viewed by the wider workforce to make your recruitment tasks of the future more efficient and more effective. In the long term it is designed to save both time and money.

Remember the end goal: the bottom line profits gained by having the best talent on the market working for you will be exponential.

PART 3
MARKETING YOUR
PROPOSITION

ONLINE PRESENCE

Showcase a careers website that attracts, converts and get results

We have established over and over again that recruiting top talent is a sales and marketing effort. Therefore, the product you are selling (your careers) needs a shop window just like anything else that you would sell. Not having a dedicated website to sell your goods or services would be crazy.

How would you expect your sales team to perform without a website? Without sales brochures? Without case studies? Without demos?

So why expect this to be any different for your recruiters?

We have looked in quite some detail at branding and how to make it stronger and more appealing to both customers and potential employees. We know that the branding for customers should be different to that for your talent community. We know that any company that wants to succeed over the next 20 years needs to prioritise attracting and retaining the top Millennial talent. We have looked at different ways of making this happen. Above all, though, there needs to be a tool that brings all of your efforts together in one place. Once you have this tool, it can be the place where you publish your content, advertise your jobs, communicate your passions and generate the next pool of applicants for any future vacancies you generate.

The place where all your content, your goals, your ideas and your inspiration should sit comfortably together is your careers website. Large companies have a careers website that sits alongside their corporate website and their company website to talk about all things careers. The successful ones contain all kinds of different things that can make their company relevant and engaging. You need your careers website to speak to your audience of potential new recruits in a language they understand.

Your careers website needs to feel relevant. Clicks through your website by people who don't stay or don't return are actually counterproductive. With a new visitor you will in all likelihood only get one chance to convert them into a regular reader. This means that your careers website needs to be immediately engaging. Visitors need to sign up and opt in to your talent community on their first visit. Time is such a precious commodity, and your visitor will not appreciate theirs being wasted.

If your social media promises a careers website that will make a difference, you'd better deliver it! You only get one chance to make the perfect impression so that takes the perfect website. The content needs to be useful to the reader. Too many careers websites are useful to the employer but not to the reader. Be different. Make your careers website do what the reader wants it to do.

One area that is now an absolute must is making sure that your website is mobile-friendly. Many websites are accessed on smartphones and your website needs to look its best on all devices. It is essential that the mobile website experience is as good as the desktop website. Don't forget that Millennials are really adept at technology and will look once and disappear from your view forever if you don't give them what they want.

Your careers website should be a single place where you can pull together all aspects of your recruitment efforts. Far from being about recruitment and nothing else, it should be the home of your visions and goals when it comes to recruiting top Millennial talent and then getting them to stay with your company for the long run. It needs to sing and dance the values that your company holds when it comes to employment. It needs to let the employment market out there know why you are so good to work for and how you can make the employment dreams of the reader come true.

It can contain hints and tips about how to become a better applicant. The company that gives an idea of their ideal applicant will be more likely to attract their ideal applicant. If people know in advance that you are looking for a certain skill, a certain character, a qualification or experience then they can go out and make that happen. The Millennial thrives on accurate information and the incentive to achieve, so if they can find out what you want from them some time before there is a position to apply for, they will go out and make things happen. Information is the key to a successful careers website and the more relevant information you can upload the better it will be received and understood.

Your careers website is a great place to house the content that we discussed earlier in the book. Your content will get your careers website seen and your careers website will get your content seen. As you write and upload relevant and interesting content it will rise up the search engine rankings and take the whole website with it. You will gain readers and followers and they will return regularly to read what you have to say. As you become an authority in your particular field of work, this will bring visitors to your careers website. While they are there you can attract them to vacancies. The higher number of quality applicants you can attract to your careers website on a regular basis the better chance you have of attracting a quality applicant and filling your vacancy with someone who will take your company forward in the future.

The way in which your company looks after its current employees is a strong indicator of how it will look after new recruits. Don't be afraid to include some case studies from current employees so that potential new recruits can see the human side of your team. It is all well and good for people to read about job specifications and ideas on what makes the perfect applicant, but there needs to be a human side to the story. We saw in a previous chapter that you current team can be great ambassadors for your company and will help to recruit new members of the team with their enthusiasm and positivity. You can extend this to your own careers website by getting your existing team to tell people what they love about their job and this will attract new talent that have a similar interest.

The specifications of every job should be searchable on your careers website. You will have many visitors, especially if you get all of the above right, so you want them to find something relevant to their life and their career. If you have career choices that people naturally gravitate to, you will want these career paths publicised on your careers website. You don't want a visitor who is looking for something to spark their interest to find nothing suitable. This would be even more heart-breaking if it turned out you did have career options that suited this visitor but didn't have the information on your site for them to make that connection. Information is king. Make sure that you have all the relevant information on the site. It may make the difference between gaining new members to your talent community or losing a visitor for them to never return.

Your careers website pulls everything about the recruitment process together. Don't be fooled into thinking that it is just a place for people to search for jobs and upload their CV in application. It must be a vibrant, energetic place where people can read the latest news from your industry and find out what you are looking for in a future applicant. It should be somewhere that your employer brand lives and breathes. Your careers website needs as much investment in terms of time and money as your other websites. Your employer branding dictates the reach that you have in the employment market and gives you the opportunity to get better applicants more quickly and at a lower cost. It is key to attracting and retaining top Millennial talent.

Top tips for creating a functional careers/recruitment website that gets results

- Follow the AIDA (Attention-Interest-Desire-Action) principle.
- Follow the '8 Second Rule' (This is the amount of time you have to engage visitors), engage quickly with a compelling Value Proposition Statement.
- Integrate your email marketing by offering value to your visitors in exchange for contact details.

- Showcase a blog and publish relevant content regularly.
- Include recruitment gamification platforms.
- Optimise your website for use on all devices including mobile & tablets.
- Integrate a functional and searchable job board to showcase live roles.
- Include engaging video content.
- Ensure that it's visually appealing and functional from a design point of view to your specific target market and that the user experience is perfect.

Build a talent community

Recruiting the best teams can be a drain on the precious assets that you have as an employer. It takes time and resources to recruit for any vacancy, whether it has been created by an expansion in your business, a higher level of trade or someone leaving your business either on a permanent or temporary basis. There are many different methods that employers have looked at when it comes to reducing the cost of recruitment and the timeframe over which a position is empty. There is a significant cost saving in advertising a vacancy through your existing team to see if they know anyone who can do the job. This does nothing, however, for your knowledge of the candidate's quality and may only end up with you starting the search again if no suitable candidate can be found via this method. It is a commonly used method in non-specialised roles such as re-tail, and this is because there can be a high turnover of staff. Headhunting is another method popular with the business owner in a hurry. A specialist job fair can sometimes bring in the right candidates but it is a hit-and-miss affair and, rather like asking your employees for recommendations, it can leave you back at square one later in the process. So what are the solutions for the more inventive companies? What if you want to find quality quickly?

A solution that some companies have started to employ to combat this longstanding problem is that of the talent pool. A talent pool is where you have a number of suitably qualified individuals that have agreed to 'stay on file' if a vacancy arises. They will have often come to your attention from prior recruitment efforts and while they may not have been given a position with you in the past for whatever reason, you may be useful to each other at some stage in the future. Having this group of individuals on your file, to a degree already vetted to confirm that they fit your requirements, is a fantastic way to keep talented individuals at easy reach. In terms of what we have looked at above, the talent pool is a cost-effective and time-efficient way of recruiting for your next vacancy. It's a great way of looking at how you recruit and how you can make the most of the tools at your disposal. But you must commit to building a remarkable proposition for talent to be interested in joining your talent pool.

The use of a talent pool keeps down the cost of hiring because it greatly reduces the likelihood that you will have to advertise your vacancy. Job adverts on general recruitment sites, specialist industry websites or in the press are usually very expensive. Any way in which you can fill a vacancy without having to spend big on these adverts is a godsend. This is why so many big employers offer their team an incentive if they recommend a friend. The incentive is large enough to get current employees interested but it is small compared with other ways of advertising a vacancy. The talent pool sidesteps this requirement in most cases. Once you have the talent on your database then they can be contacted without cost whenever there is a vacancy. This puts you in total control and you will hear back from those interested without the need to spend on advertising. All you need to do is to send out an email to those who are suited to the role you have available. The regular communication that this involves also keeps potential applicants of the future curious about hearing more. This means that your next vacancy, and the one after that, have already got potential applicants sitting there waiting to hear about it.

Although recommendations from existing team members for vacancies will not always work, the fact is that recommendations for talent pool members can be a good idea. As you are working in advance of the vacancies appearing,this will give you time to assess and vet the potential applicants long before of any recruitment process. If, on the other hand, you rely on your team to provide you new recruits immediately then you may end up not getting very far.

The talent pool is also incredibly helpful when it comes to reducing the amount of time it takes to generate responses. Every day that you have an unfilled vacancy is a day that you could have been generating more income, a day that your customers may notice a drop in service. The time it takes you to fill a vacancy should be one of the measures you use of how efficient you are in this area of business. Many potential employees are already tied to contracts with a long notice period. It is the norm to wait for one month, three months or even six months until your preferred candidate works their notice period. So you need to keep the time it takes you to make a decision to an absolute minimum. If you are able to advertise to your talent pool and start to hear back from interested parties straight away, you have sidestepped the time of waiting for a print run, the lengthy timescale you need to give to closing dates or any of the other time-consuming extras that are part of the usual frustration when advertising via traditional methods.

So if the way forward is to build a talent pool, how do you get there? The first step is to start this process with your most recent job vacancies. You can start to go back to previous applicants and ask if they want to remain on your file to be considered for future roles. This gives you an immediate talent pool to start prospecting when the next job becomes available.

You will need a section on your careers website for people to register for the talent pool. It doesn't have to cost much to develop, but a tool that invites people to enter their details and perhaps add a CV will dripfeed you with talent that wants to work for you. If you can get people to come to you you will be looking at potential applicants that have visited your website, looked around and decided it is something that they want to be considered for in the future. You already have someone who wants to work with you.

Talent magnets

Imagine that you have access to a list of interested potential recruits in your target market, who have already given you permission to approach them when an opportunity arises. A great way to implement this is to create, for each of your growing divisions, '**Talent Magnets**' that are created specifically for your target market.

How do you get the contact details of interested parties to add to your email list? You offer them something of value or interest in exchange for their details. You also ask permission to keep them posted on updates in the future. This is known as permission marketing and it is a highly effective way to recruit into your talent pool.

First, you create relevant content and information for your market to publish on your careers site and social media channels. If you want to increase your talent pool of graduates for your sales division for example, think about what information they would like to get their hands on.

- Take our test: Have you got what it takes to be our next sales superstar?
- Free E-guide! 10 tips for ambitious graduates to progress their career in sales.
- Free Report. Find out how 'John Smith' progressed from a Graduate Trainee to Sales Director with our firm in 5 years.

You get the drift. Offer something that sparks interest in your target market. Get their contact details, gain permission and add value to them with relevant content.

Recruiting is a sales process! Just like sales, people won't buy into your company unless they know you, like you and trust you. These things don't happen overnight.

It's good to build separate landing and squeeze pages throughout your careers website for each of your divisions. This way your offering can be bespoke to each of your target markets. Tech content for your IT division, Digital Media content to attract talent for your Marketing division, and so on.

If you know you are expecting a recruitment drive for one of your divisions, you will need to add fresh talent and interest to the talent pool ahead of time. The best way to do this is to utilise pay-per-click (PPC) and targeted marketing on the landing pages of your career site.

You can target the specific talent you need on social media such as LinkedIn, Facebook and Twitter. Generally speaking, LinkedIn is likely to be the most beneficial due to the niche demographics you can aim your marketing to. Below are some examples on the demographics you can target your marketing efforts to:

- Job Title
- Location
- Skills
- Education
- Interests

Mass media advertising is dead: gone are the days of advertising in media outlets such as general newspapers hoping that at least a small percentage of readers include your target market. Hone in on your target market and own your niche.

Gamification

Culture match tests. Technical games. Video elevator pitches. Knowledge tests. Psychometric games. Personality quizzes.

Richard Evans

There are many ways in which you can look at your recruitment to decide how to filter a pool of candidates down. The use of gamification in recruitment is just starting to take hold and it is a great way of testing the skills of applicants and selecting the candidate that is right for your business. Gamification means using the techniques and dynamics of a game and applying them to other areas of life and business – in this case applying them to recruitment. Your average Millennial will enjoy the challenge that this sets them and you will get the best out of your potential recruits if you challenge their skills in this environment. It is a great way to motivate people to show off their skill set in a recruitment scenario and can beat the traditional interview for actually seeing behaviours and skills rather than just talking about them.

When someone starts to look through the job market at their options they are more attracted to dynamic and innovative employers. If you are an employer that uses gamification as part of your recruitment you will stand out, and immediately become more attractive to those that are looking for employment. When looking to attract and retain the top Millennial talent you want to give them a challenge that keeps them on top of their game and stimulates their need to be engaged and interested in their work. You as an employer suddenly jump to the top of the Millennial's attention because you offer something exciting and different. It sparks the curiosity of most of the people out there looking for a new job.

This is especially true if you are working in an industry that requires problem solving on a regular basis, or needs creative and dynamic individuals. As this covers most businesses in most industries, gamification becomes a recruitment tool that can help most companies out there. It is especially useful if you have a high number of candidates for any particular role and you want to effectively reduce this to a workable number.

Gamification allows you to get potential applicants to compete against each other so you end up with the best applicants. As you have implemented the strategies in this book you will start to see the results of a larger talent pool and a higher number of applicants for each job role that you advertise. This is a problem in itself (but a nice problem to have). Part of the solution to the problem is to employ gamification as part of your recruitment and selection process to get this larger number of applicants down to the quality core that you want to select your next new recruit from.

The Millennial will automatically be inspired and interested in a recruitment process that involves gamification because they have grown up around video games. They have a natural skill set that matches the requirements gamification sets. This is where your game will dictate the results that you get. There are specialist companies out there that will set up and deliver gamification recruitment programs that will allow you to select the candidates that most closely fit the profile you are looking for. The skills and behaviours that you require need to be carefully thought-out in advance so you are getting the results you need for your business.

There are some simple steps that you can take immediately at low cost to instil some gamification in your recruitment process.

You could check out skills with online tests

In recruitment you sometimes need a way of reducing the number of applicants to a manageable level quickly. By setting tests, puzzles and tasks, you can get your pool of applicants into shape. These do two things: first, they make you a more fun and attractive employer to work for. Potential new recruits automatically are drawn to your company when they are looking for an employer. Second, you get to see the skills that you require in action. You can see how someone performs rather than hear them tell you how they perform.

There was a big shift in recruitment around 20 years ago when interviewers started asking competency-based questions. It was designed to get to the core of behaviour by finding specific examples of how the applicants had performed in the past. Gamification is the next level where you can actually see how the applicants perform in a test situation.

Video elevator pitches

Video elevator pitches give you more of a glimpse into the personality of a candidate than a CV ever will. Once you have a FaceTime or Skype connection you can get straight on to interviewing applicants over the internet without having to meet face-to-face. You then have a video record of how they performed rather than relying on the notes that you took at the time. It makes collective decisions on hiring far easier to reach because all stakeholders can see how they reacted and performed.

You could create a virtual job fair

If you recruit from a diverse geographic area then you may struggle to find a presence that is effective at more traditional job fairs offline. But a virtual job fair can be a great way to attract the right people to your company. It gives something different and new, and potential applicants are immediately attracted to this innovation. It gives you a chance to have a two-way conversation with people: you give out details about your company, your vacant positions and your careers website, and in return you get potential candidates coming to you and you can collect details to add them to your email subscribers list, direct them to your talent pool or get them to apply for the positions you have available.

You could keep people up to date

Gamification appears in many areas of internet life, and one such way that keeps up the interest levels is a way of updating your applicants on their progress. If they complete the application form, for example, they reach level 1; the second stage could be called level 2; and so on, all the way up to the interview, which might be called the 'Boss Level'. By using the language that the Millennial is familiar with you are talking on their level and they are more attracted to you as a company. If you add in prizes such as special offers or exclusive content when they reach higher levels it all becomes a part of the game. The challenge in itself will attract more quality applicants.

Gamification, or certain aspects of it, is a great way to assess the suitability of applicants and to appear as a forward-thinking company. You will appear more attractive in the eyes of potential

Millennial recruits because you become the innovative company that thinks about how they can recruit, rather than following the norm. You get to make your recruitment process more fun for both sides and you can see real-life skills in action. Overall, there is a move to more remote recruitment practices and testing applicants with assessments to get a smaller group of relevant and qualified applicants. These measures make the process more interesting and are more cost-effective for your recruitment of the top Millennial talent. Once you have identified exactly what you want to measure, you can ask the right questions and find the right results.

Develop a mobile recruitment app

Technology continues apace in all areas of life, and recruitment is no different. To be able to attract the top Millennial talent you need to produce new and innovative ways of engaging your audience and retaining their interest. The latest developments have married the functionality of the dating app with the more traditional job listings website to produce something that users love because it is easy to use and produces results fast. Don't forget that one of the defining characteristics of the Millennial generation is that they use technology to get the answers they want quickly. It is only a good thing for your recruitment if you have a functional and quality mobile recruitment app for your end-users to utilise when they are looking for their next job role.

It is said that more than half of all those looking for a job will search on a smartphone or tablet; this figure will only be higher in the Millennial generation that has grown up using technology in their everyday life. The use of a mobile recruitment app will put your company at the front of the queue when people are looking for their next employer because it shows a dedication to excellence and an understanding of technology that will set you apart from other recruiters. The app, like your website, will give information about the roles you have available 24 hours a day, 7 days a week, every week of the year. It is able to give information and attract talent whether your company is open or closed. You can directly communicate with your potential applicants without the need for costly verbal communication in the first instance and without the need for costly recruitment agencies. The great recruitment apps are still to be developed so it is a good time to get into the market and produce something that blows your competition away. Here's what a great recruitment app should look like and do.

It needs to work hard for recruiters AND applicants

The app needs to fulfil a need on both sides of the equation – that of the recruiters and the applicants. It won't survive if it just serves the purpose of only one side, because it won't get the users from the other side that makes it worthwhile. Developing an app is about far more than just the technology involved. You could commission a recruitment app from any number of developers but if you don't understand what it needs to do and communicate this effectively you will have no hope of making the right app. It needs to provide enough information to the applicants in order for them to make a decision about which jobs to apply for. It needs to provide enough information about the applicants so that the recruiter can make a decision about whose application to progress. The clever recruitment app needs to do this in a way that doesn't overload either side with needless information. So it is a balancing act to make sure that both sides are happy.

Richard Evans

It needs to be user-friendly

This is an absolute must because the best apps are those that are easy to understand and easy to use. The simple swipe that has been borrowed from the dating apps is a great way to get people to understand immediately what you want them to do. If they swipe left then the job opportunity is discarded and if you swipe right then it goes into a "yes" pile. What happens next is also crucial because if that "yes" pile just sits on the app then it might get lost forever. You could generate an email with all of the jobs put into the "yes" pile in one visit to the app so that the user is prompted to follow that through by reading more or making a full application.

Add the extras

Your app needs to cover the basics as outlined above but there is so much more that you as a recruiter wants to know about your potential applicants, so there is scope to add extras. If you allow people to upload a short video resume or answer some specific questions then you will gain a further insight into those using your app and whether they are suited to your company. You can learn a lot here from LinkedIn because they encourage people to add more information rather than force them to. Every time you log on it tells you how complete your profile is and you feel encouraged to add a little more to make the percentage increase. Your app can encourage people to add more and this means that they are more engaged with the app and you get the benefit of more information to enable a decision to be made. The more information that is uploaded, the better your results will be because you will have access to more accurate information about your prospects.

Different channels

Your app is one way of getting people more engaged with your recruitment efforts and your employer brand. But, as with all recruitment, the more multi-channel you can make it the more effective it will become. Your social media can promote your app and your app can promote your social media. All should link back to your careers page. The underlying messages here are twofold. First, make sure that you can reach as many people as possible by being in all the right places. Second, you need to have engaging content. A list of words on a page of what a job is all about will eventually be replaced by videos explaining the job so you need to ensure that your content is engaging from the outset. The thought of a new job is exciting for anyone. What fills people with dread is reading through job descriptions, filling out application forms and fighting through recruitment websites. If your app can make this process quicker and easier, your Millennial applicants will love you forever. They just want an easy life and a quick result.

Give relevant notifications

The power of the mobile app has been multiplied by the notification settings on most smartphones. It allows the app developer to send relevant information to the person who has downloaded the app. Those people that have downloaded a recruitment app may look at it every now and again if they are searching for a job. Those that just have the app on their smartphone will be far more likely to use the app and apply for your jobs if they get a relevant notification when a suitable job is posted. This is multiplying the power of the app by engaging the passive user as well as the active user.

A mobile app to promote your jobs and enhance the perception of your employer brand is a great way to develop the way that you recruit. Once you are able to engage your prospects on the move and send them push notifications when something relevant comes up then you will get access to a greater number of applicants. This will drive up the number of people that you reach with any new vacancy and should drive up the quality of applicants because you are reaching more people and gathering better information on them. Every area that you improve with regards to your recruitment efforts is a step in the right direction to becoming more effective and more efficient in your search for new team members for your company. The average Millennial will be found much more easily on their smartphone than in any other area of life so you need to put yourself in a position where they can find you.

INTERNAL PRESENCE

Implement an employee referral scheme that works

Your employee referral scheme is a great way to engage your team in finding the talent that can help your company get to the next level. This can be an important method of finding quality new recruits without great expense of time. But you need to get it right in order for it to be operating at maximum effect.

Make the program visible

You need your team to know all about it, because without visibility there will be no response from your existing team. The launch of the programme is a fantastic place to start because the publicity you can give it on that occasion will embed the programme in the minds of your team. This is also the time to set out the strategy that you will use during the promotion of the referral scheme. Like everything you do this is most effective if it's well-planned. Regular reminders in places such as email footers, social media and payslips will jog the memory of your team, and help you attract like-minded Millennial talent to your organisation. It makes recruitment more cost-effective and takes less time than the traditional route of advertising externally. Along with the visibility of the programme you need to make sure that the rules regarding referrals are clear and easy to understand. The worst referral schemes have pages of rules that nobody understands and thus get no interest from the team. The best schemes have a few rules that are easy to comprehend and thus get buy-in from existing employees because they know what they have to do to qualify.

Make sure the referral is treated as important

If the referral isn't acknowledged and fast-tracked, the employee may wonder why they took the time to make it. Your hiring department must get in touch with the person who made the referral, preferably face-to-face, to thank them personally for their introduction. It means so much more when this happens, because the existing team member understands how important it is to the business. Also, be sure to get in touch with the person referred as soon as possible. This process is about bypassing a lot of the rigmarole that goes with recruitment and making the process faster and more efficient. Don't lose this efficiency by letting the potential applicant or the existing employee think that they have been forgotten as the wheels of the normal recruitment process grind on. At the other end of the process, the payment must be swift and painless for the existing employee. The criteria for the employee to receive a reward should be clearly stated at every stage, and there should be no reason for the existing employee to have to chase up the payment or enquire about the status of it. An automated system that pays out when criteria have been met is the simplest way to achieve this.

What are the rewards?

The most effective employee referral schemes are about much more than the money on offer. The building of trust and interest in you as an employer is just as valuable for you as for the new recruit.

The acknowledgement that someone has done a good job in referring talent to the company means a lot to the existing employee as well. Although a cash reward is the most common method of recognising the referral, there are other ways of highlighting the positive contribution that a team member has made. If a team member is congratulated for their referral by a business leader in the presence of their peers, this is incredibly empowering and can start a chain of similar referrals in the future. Think about how you reward your team in this respect and you can maximise the results. This can be extended to the running of competitions between employees, teams or departments to see who can provide the most referrals over a certain period of time. This is especially useful if you are looking to fill many vacancies at once because it will get people thinking about who they know, and making a more conscious effort to refer people to you.

When to get referrals in

There can be a tendency to only accept referrals when you are actively recruiting. But this means that you have to switch the awareness of the scheme on and off whenever necessary. It involves more work to re-launch the scheme on a regular basis than to keep a high level of awareness all the time. So you need to consider accepting referrals on an ongoing basis. If the people involved in the referral are kept informed of the situation then they will understand that the application may not be acted upon immediately but they will be assessed and kept on file for a potential future opportunity. This means that you get to grow your talent pool at all times and can act quickly when a suitable vacancy arises within your company. Then the normal procedures that relate to the employee referral scheme can re-start as normal.

The whole picture for the whole team

You must change the culture in your company with regards the referral of talent. Once you get every employee from every department on board, you start to build a referral culture. You employees' emotional investment in your business means more than just getting new recruits faster and cheaper than other methods; they are expanding your reach as an employer. They are saying to their friends and family, 'This is an employer that I am so proud to work for that I recommend you work here too.' The positive impact this has on your employer brand is amazing. You create company advocates because your employees understand how important they are to your business and your future. Once you have developed that great employer brand and communicated your values effectively to your existing team, they will become more effective referrers for you. When they understand what makes the company tick, they will be better placed to pass on that message. This makes every member of your team a potential referrer because they get the big picture about where the organisation is going. Remember: the average Millennial wants to work somewhere that they feel makes a positive impact on the world. Well, they also want their peers to know that they are making a positive impact, so when they communicate this they are generating future referrals to your company.

Communicate effectively internally with a functional social intranet platform

All companies need to ensure that the lines of communication are open at every level. To keep up team morale you need to give employees an outlet to engage them and give them an area for company communication and for the workforce to engage with each other. This is what a social intranet does, and the benefits it can have for your company are interesting. Traditional company intranets are sites that are stuffed full of information by every department. They tend to be useful for specific information, but are often hard to navigate. This means that they become ignored and unused, so the effort and expense involved goes to waste. The modern equivalent that smart companies are using is the social intranet that borrows features from social media to make it a dynamic and engaging place to share ideas and collaborate. The idea grew in stature and prominence after publication of *The Cluetrain Manifesto,* which espoused a multi-directional flow of knowledge, rather than the traditional top-down dictation of information. But what is a social internet? How does it work for your company? What does it do to help you attract and retain the top Millennial talent? Let's take a look.

The social intranet

This uses all of the information that you can usually find on an intranet and adds the feature of allowing team members to message each other across departments and across sites. This is beyond email: it is more akin to a social network where people can add to articles with likes, comments and shares. Procedures can be streamlined or improved when a team member adds a great idea to an existing intranet article or a tip on how to use a piece of information. The social intranet is part forum, part social network, part information source, and entirely useful. When the employees of your company engage with the content and start to see the benefit of contributing then they become bigger advocates of your company (including the employer brand), and more productive. The innovative company social intranets allow people to form groups, so the collaborative approach to solving problems comes to the forefront of the organisation's work practice. Don't forget that Millennials are collaborative workers and by enabling the average Millennial to work in this way you are appealing to their sense of community. This helps you to attract and retain the top talent from the Millennial generation as they feel more closely linked to your company as an employer. The development of a company social intranet goes straight to the core of an employee's need to feel valued and be part of something. By enabling team members to contribute to discussions and add their input to solve problems or help others you are creating a feeling of belonging to the company that is a powerful tool in retaining your existing team.

Further uses

The rise of technology has been credited with both bringing people together and driving people apart in everyday life. When used in the right way in business it is a great tool for crossing large distances. A department can record a short video message about a new product launch or initiative and upload it to the social intranet in a matter of minutes. This means that this information can travel great distances across the company in a very short space of time. The impact of a personal video message from a key stakeholder in the business is a powerful tool that far outweighs the impact a written message or email might have. This is another way the social intranet is changing companies for the better. It allows each department head to bring the internal brand together across one platform so the company can work towards the shared vision. It is another extension of the customer brand and the employer brand because it allows everyone in the organisation to see the vision and values that are driving the company forward. These are just some of the applications for the social intranet; you can run competitions, ask for photos of people in the workplace or allow some of the non-sensitive content to be shared on social media outlets - and the sharing of information is always good for business.

Direct applications for recruitment

There are some direct applications for the social intranet that can help you in the search for new employees that will take your company forward. It is a great place to launch the employee referral scheme that we looked at in a previous chapter. The social intranet can allow you to inform people of the scheme, give details of the rules and give access to the link that they can make the referral on. It is a great enabler and gets the vital exposure that your employee referral scheme needs to thrive. For new starters there is the option to create groups so they can work together through any initial challenges. It gives people a voice in the company as soon as they start and allows people to share experiences and bounce ideas off each other. This is a great way to extend and improve the on-boarding process as it makes the new recruits feel as though they are a part of something bigger. As you develop the social intranet to include more and more areas of your business it becomes a working tool for these new recruits as well. They can access the information that has been uploaded and then have the option to ask questions about it, share it to their new starter group and make other uses of it. The document that was initially uploaded as a source of information now becomes a living and breathing part of the company.

Input on to the social intranet

It would be tempting to put the content of the social intranet into the hands of the people that put together your company's old-style intranet, but this kind of defeats the object of it. There should be a broad base of people that can upload information. When you trust people to use the system in a mature and relevant manner they generally do just that. Any unnecessary or unacceptable content will be quickly identified and reported by other users so it can be removed from the intranet as soon as possible. If you want the intranet to be engaging and dynamic then you need to let people upload relevant and engaging content. It will then become the place where your entire company hangs out to share the best working practices and all the information they feel that the rest of the company can benefit from. When it becomes something that is owned by the team then it will become something that is used and valued by the team. Let go of the reins a little and get the most out of the social intranet. It will give your team a fresh outlook on the company and will help you to attract and retain the top Millennial talent.

Your company is full of vibrant and engaging people that are capable of doing their own jobs and inspiring each other. The social intranet is the place where these people can meet and drive your company forward. By having something in place that inspires your wider team and helps them to feel valued you will create a sum that is greater than the parts. The ability to collaborate, ask questions and develop relationships across divisions, departments and locations is a hugely enabling tool that will cement your place as the employer of choice in your industry.

DIGITAL MARKETING

Engage and promote via email marketing

Email marketing is big business. When done correctly, such as in the way Amazon uses it, it can generate huge sales to genuine prospects.

Customers prefer to receive communication by email and respond in large numbers to specific offers or deals. The impact of a good email marketing strategy can be massive because you have a group of people that have elected to receive communication from your company and are actually waiting to hear from you.

In terms of recruitment this is absolute gold. It is a natural extension of both your talent pool and your careers website. Getting it right means a lot, so we will take a look at setting up your email marketing and how this can impact the success of your recruitment, including growing your employer brand. When someone browses your careers website, applies for a job with you or joins your talent pool, what do you do with their information? Do you just hold it on file for future use? Or do you ask their permission to keep in touch? It would be great to be able to pick up the phone to each of these people every few weeks and see how they are, but this is time-consuming and expensive. But by sending them a regular email you can stay in touch and build your reputation in their Eyes.

This will be done through the use of an email service provider.

There are many review websites for the various options out there now, so take a look at the providers' reputation and the services they offer. You want them to be reliable and to give you great customer service. Ask your peers for any recommendations or providers to avoid. Selecting your email service provider is like selecting any other member of your team. The best provider will bring you the best results.

Start by thinking about what you actually want for your email marketing. You will have a certain number of subscribers in mind, so you need to establish how you are going to collect these subscribers. You can sign them up from your careers website, ask permission from all those who apply for jobs you advertise and leverage your social media to ask for subscribers.

YouTube is another great way to attract subscribers. Make the most of your presence wherever it is. You will have a good idea of how many subscribers are useful to you from the number of jobs you normally advertise in a given year. You know how many applicants you want to attract to each vacancy so from there you can get a broad idea of how many subscribers you want. It is useful to set a target number of subscribers for the first year, to become your measure of success.

The easiest way to win in this area is to set up a subscribe form on your website. Something along the lines of 'Do you like what you see? Want more tips on how to write the perfect job application? Then sign up here for our weekly email.' This turns the casual viewer into someone that has given you their permission to be contacted every week. You can build a list of people that want to hear from you.

This is invaluable for attracting and retaining the top Millennial talent because you will find the average Millennial on their smartphone, checking their email or social media accounts regularly. As long as the content is fresh and interesting, you have someone who grows to know and like your employer brand.

You have a potential applicant that will now be raring to work for you. If you tap into the Millennial need to make a difference and to work for an employer that values them, you are immediately onto a winner.

You can multiply the effect of the subscribe form by prompting people from other sources to sign up too. If all your social media recruitment marketing is designed to return your readers to your careers website then maybe a pop-up as the site is first entered is a good way to get interested parties to subscribe to the information you send out. You can use special offers to leverage the number of subscribers. Any offer of a free e-book or some valuable content to subscribers will more than likely get you more subscribers than just asking for people to sign up. It is human nature that people are more moved by the offer of something free than they are by the offer of information.

Richard Evans

Think about all the places that your company is seen and where you would like to convert users into subscribers. Try to get that message across in all of these Places.

Once you have put steps in place to grow your subscribers you need to contact them. There are a few basic messages that you need to get across to all of your subscribers in the early days before you establish an ongoing line of communication. It is all about easing your subscribers into the flow of messages that you will deliver in the future. The first message should be a confirmation message. It is quite disconcerting for people when they aren't absolutely certain that they have subscribed. The confirmation email will reassure the subscriber that they have opted to receive your messages and removes the element of doubt.

The next message will be the welcome message thanking them for subscribing and delivering any offers that you promised. The most important part of the welcome message is to outline what they have subscribed to. It should briefly explain the frequency of the emails and the content of the emails that they will receive. As with all other forms of marketing it is important that you are delivering the right messages to the relevant people. If someone has signed up specifically for the special offers you have promised but would never be in a position to apply for one of your vacancies, it may be just as well that they opt out of the email marketing now. You want as many subscribers as you can get, but you will only gain value from those that will be in a position to apply with you in the future. The welcome message gives the new subscriber the information they need to understand where things will go from here.

96

After this it is a case of setting up and sending regular emails that will create the ongoing communication with your prospects and nurture the relationship. You need to remember what it was that you promised in the first place. If, as in the example above, you said that you would send tips on how to create the perfect job application, this is what you need to email out. The regular emails will form the backbone of your relationship with your subscribers. Your messages will become the promotion of your employer brand with this group and you can use this forum to communicate your values and ideals. As this grows over time you will have people that will jump at the chance to apply for any job vacancies you advertise in the future. You get a ready-made talent pool that has asked to be kept informed about what you have to say.

There will be times when your emails don't follow the usual patterns that you have established above; when there is something special or different to say - mainly when you have a vacancy. These vacancy announcement emails are when you want to deliver a quick message and elicit a response.

The message in these emails needs to be very clear and the content will be much shorter than usual. You want your audience to know that you have a job vacancy and then to click through to the details on your careers website. Make sure that you capture their attention and give a clear call to action. This is when you convert your subscribers into potential new recruits. The hard work that you have put in so far can pay off here.

The content of your emails

The content in your emails won't be well-received if it is just full of talk about how great your company is. Although the end objective is to get people to want to work for you, you need to be much more subtle about how you achieve this. People want to subscribe to an email every week because they get something out of it. You need to produce something that has them staying on as subscribers and enhancing your employer brand every single week. There are several ways in which you can do this. Keeping people informed about the latest news in your industry is a way to gain subscribers and keep up the interest levels. The readers that you want will be in your industry already or interested in your industry. If you can give them new and engaging content about this industry then they will stay tuned in.

Alternatively, you can give people ideas and tips about their perfect job application. These work for both parties: you are telling subscribers how to give you a better application. They will read every week because they are getting information that can help them. You will be getting a readership that wants to see what you tell them next. This gives your employer brand a massive lift because you are seen as a company that looks after people whether they work for you or not. Don't forget that the average Millennial wants to work for an employer that has similar values to them and they want to feel as though they make a difference. If your company is making a difference to the lives and job prospects of their subscribers then you will be better able to attract and retain Millennial talent.

Designing your emails

It's important to consider the visual impact of your emails.

The first consideration is the branding. We know how important consistency is across your employer branding and the email is no exception. If someone doesn't recognise it as coming from the company they subscribed to, you may lose them straight away. Your logo, placed prominently, will give the reader an immediate confirmation of who you are. Like much of marketing, too many words can be a real killer. You need to break it up with images, charts, graphs or other visual aids. The email that is full of words will not get the same response as those that have something visual to enhance the way they look and feel.

Another way to enhance this effect is to break up the text in other ways. The use of colour, text in different sizes, bullet points, capitals, bold and underlined text are all great ways of making sure that everything in your email looks and feels different to the subscriber. Every way in which you can make the email feel less like just a series of connected words is a positive move in terms of retaining subscribers and getting them to read what you have written.

The other really big consideration here is how the email is structured. With the best will in the world, you will not get every reader to get to the bottom of every email you send. This just does not happen. So the most important information needs to be at the top of the email. This is the part that all your readers will see.

The last consideration is the time of day that you send these emails. You will probably have a readership that is largely within your own country. You will want to hit your subscribers at a time that suits them so you need to make sure that it arrives in their email inbox at an opportune time.

Start with the time that you feel works best but you can monitor the success of these emails and adjust as you see necessary.

Measuring the performance of your emails

As part of the programme from your email service provider you will see data on how the email has performed. It will show you how many subscribers clicked through, which content was most successful and who went on to spend time on your careers website. When you know what is working well, you can give your readers more of it. When you know what your readers don't respond to, you know what to eliminate. This is an ongoing process of improvement.

As your subscriber profile changes the content that they want to read may change as well.

Don't forget to look at people that unsubscribe too. There will inevitably be some people who no longer want to receive your emails. This is not a disaster. Of course you'd rather keep all your subscribers, but you only want followers that are getting something out of it. Don't be afraid to ask those who unsubscribe why they are leaving. You want to understand what is making people leave your mailing list because when you understand it you can do something to prevent it in future. This is a constant process of re-evaluation, because the smart recruiter stays ahead of the game at all times instead of reacting after the fact.

Engage with relevant content marketing via your blogs

Engaging with your talent market through content marketing is a tool that forward-thinking recruiters should embrace. It's a proven success. You can connect with potential new employees and build a relationship that you can nurture over the longer term. When you are ready to recruit, these people will be more likely to apply for the vacancy you advertise because they know you, hopefully like you and have built up a level of trust.

Recruitment changes every day, thanks to technology. Social media and the internet make mass communication fast and cost-effective. You now need to think like a marketer and blogger as well as thinking like a recruiter. SEO counts.

POTENTIAL BENEFITS OF CONTENT MARKETING FOR YOUR RECRUITERS

It generates website clicks

Google loves new and relevant content. By having relevant content with the right keywords in the right frequency you will get your careers site noticed and move it up the search engine rankings. When you have a job to advertise you want it to appear as high as possible on the search pages. Having relevant content helps you to achieve this.

It is cost-efficient and effective

It can be costly if you pay for clicks through a search engine such as Google. Your content will help you naturally rise up the rankings so you don't have to spend the money on doing it artificially. Millennials who work in your industry will keep informed about your industry. By having relevant content in the right places you will gain exposure from the next set of potential applicants for your next vacancy. Use LinkedIn, Twitter, Facebook and any other social media outlets to ensure that your word gets out there.

If you can feed your industry with relevant and interesting news and ideas on a regular basis then you will be the recruiter of choice when Millennials in your industry decide to look for their next opportunity.

It generates a bigger brand marketing presence

We have seen that your brand is all-important. A cheap and effective way to get your brand out there is to produce content that gets you seen. By writing relevant content and marketing it effectively on social media you have a ready-made audience that will grow into a pool of potential applicants whenever you have a new position available.

The effect of providing quality readable content is that others can easily share it. When someone reads and likes your post, the reader's contacts will be informed. This can start off a chain reaction as the work you produce gains more readers. Don't forget that Millennials spend a lot of time on social media and share what they like with their peers.

Managing your communication

The content you produce needs to be kept fresh and up to date. You need to manage your social media accounts in the same way that you manage all of your communication because it is another face of your company. For some social media users this will be the only communication they have with your company. Make sure it is a good interaction that enhances their impression of your business.

There is a lot of competition for the time of your potential recruits. So don't waste the little time you have with them. Repeats of content you have already posted or out of date information will only cause Millennials to bypass you next time. Make sure that you post information that means something to the reader more than it does to you.

Attracting prospective candidates

The point of advertising vacancies on social media is to get a response. Measure the response you are getting and make sure that you get the best from it. If you are not getting the type of response you hoped for, you may need to revisit your strategy here. There is a lot of competition for the best talent so you need to ensure that your content is relevant and easily understood.

When you have a regular line of communication open with many people in your industry you are on the road to making your recruitment efforts more efficient and streamlined. If you send regular emails to a particular group and get good feedback then this may be the group that your next new recruit comes from. Keep the lines of communication open and respond to any requests for information. If the people in your industry are talking to you and about you then you will have an easier time when it comes to attracting candidates in the future.

All of this revolves around trust. If you treat people's time with care, and any information they give you with confidentiality, you become one of the trusted sources of information in your industry. When this happens people will naturally move towards you in their career thinking and treasure more highly any job opening with you over those with your rivals.

How do you create content marketing that wins you a better quality and quantity of applicant for your next vacancy?

The book *Epic Content Marketing* by Joe Pulizzi looks at six principles of content marketing and how they fit together to help you with your business.

1. Fill a need
2. Be consistent
3. Be human
4. Have a point of view
5. Avoid sales speak
6. Be best of breed

Own your niche by following these steps and position yourself as a go-to expert.

Not all the words that your company produces every day should be considered as your content. The content marketing element is only those words that talks to your potential applicants of the future. Millennials are adept at social media so they can spot the difference between a sales pitch and something that is genuinely helpful. The key is to tell a story, to share an idea or to give advice.

The idea behind content marketing is to build a connection with your audience. This will keep you at the forefront of their mind. Whether it is buying a new watch or looking for a new job, the connection that you and that prospect have made is invaluable. It means that they come to you for answers. Joe Pulizzi emphasises this principle as a key one on the road to becoming epic in content marketing.

The reader of your content wants to get something in return for their time. This can be:

- A freebie
- A piece of information that they didn't know
- Something to pique their interest
- Knowledge that can help them

Your communication needs to be relevant and consistent. Your reader will build up a profile of you and expect something similar every time they interact with you. If they signed up for your content because they like what you give them, changing it might drive them away. You need to provide your reader with what they signed up for or the trust in your communication goes out of the window and you risk losing them forever. When looking to attract and retain the top Millennial talent the key is to broaden your sphere of influence, not to narrow it.

Millennials know how to use the internet better than any other generation. The content you provide needs to resonate in a way that nothing else does. You need to write something unique that the reader can't get anywhere else. This means that your advice and information becomes indispensable because it does something that nobody else's does. It doesn't have to be ground breaking, but it does have to have a USP so you stand out. The internet is full of content. What is going to make someone read yours?

Your company identity can really come out through the content you publish. If you stand for something different or want to let the world know your ideals, content helps you get the word out there. Don't end up with bland content because you are afraid of offending potential clients or recruits. If your company has points of view, express them.

Make sure that the content you write is just that content. Don't get caught up trying to sell everything your company offers new recruits through the medium of content marketing. That's not what it's about, and it won't win you friends. The content you produce should be efficient and meaningful, not full of sales messages.

Over time, the content you produce should be of as high quality as you can make it. Once you have started to produce high-quality content on a regular basis you will be the place to go for the people who operate in your industry. You want to become an authority on all matters that mean something in your industry and the way to do this is to show your authority through your content. Joe Pulizzi calls this 'becoming recognized as the best of its breed'.

Making it happen

You can, and should, communicate with your customers and your potential applicants in a variety of ways. So many of these methods are free to use and can be accessed at any time of the day or night by you and your potential market. As Joe Pulizzi might say, 'Make sure that your content is epic!'

Engage with video marketing

The Millennial grew up in the information age: they know how to use and manipulate tools such as social media to find what they want in the shortest amount of time possible. A Millennial has a concentrated attention span. They want to get the information they need as quickly as possible and then apply this information to their own life. From here, they can successfully manoeuvre to the next task in a very short space of time. This attention span can have good and bad aspects. For anyone looking at attracting Millennials to their company they must find a quick way of capturing their attention and an equally quick and engaging way of delivering information.

According to Cisco, video will account for 69% of all consumer internet traffic by 2017 and YouTube alone receives more than 1 billion unique visitors each month. Video marketing is a great way of engaging Millennials because it speaks their language. With the advent of tablets and smartphones, video marketing is even more powerful and even more important to your employer brand as you seek to attract and retain the top Millennial talent. The power and reach of videos is actually increasing, so they are a crucial marketing tool when looking to fill a vacancy. There are a few reasons why you should engage in video marketing, and all of them enhance the employer brand that you have.

The saying goes that a picture paints a thousand words. Well, a short video is made up of a thousand pictures so the power of this form of engagement is potentially huge. Great video marketing conveys feelings and emotions that words can't always capture. Videos are easily and widely shared on social media and can get your name out there fast when it comes to reaching out to potential new recruits. We have looked at the benefits of having a larger pool of recruits to choose from when it comes to filling your next vacancy. Video marketing is one of the tools you can use to reach a wider market. A great video will show off what your company believes in. The values of a company are really important to a Millennial because they want to work in an environment where they feel valued and that they are making a difference. Your video marketing for your employer brand needs to highlight these values.

Video helps to improve your search engine ranking. When Google, Bing, Yahoo and the others look at how to rank web pages in order of relevance to their searchers, video is taken into account. Because there are fewer sites with video than there are with text, your video will help you to move up the search rankings and be found by potential employees. This again widens your talent pool and gets you a better quality of candidate for your future job vacancies.

There are many options for making your company marketing video. The better production you can afford, the more appealing your website will look to potential employees, but the message is far more important than the money you spend on putting it together. You should concentrate on relaying your values and the way you work as a company. This will speak to the right people because they will be people that share your values. The Millennial gravitates towards organisations that best match their own view on how the world should work. Your video is an enhancement of everything else that your company does in its everyday life. It should show what you do and how you do it and be part of the bigger package of your employer brand.

There are examples of companies that do this in a good way, and a few that do it badly. Many videos are used as recruitment tools that sit alongside the rest of the careers website to complete the picture of what it would be like to work for a particular company. Big brands show current employees to let future employees know what they have in store for them. An enthusiastic existing employee is a great asset to your employer brand and can bring in more applicants from their network to apply for your next job role. If you want to attract Millennials then you should be featuring Millennials in your video marketing if you are going to make a video like this.

It doesn't just have to be a generic video that talks about your employer brand. You can use video marketing to highlight a particular vacancy. There are some great ideas out there for short videos about a particular job. Tech companies are great at using their own in-house talent to produce short engaging video content that gets applications flooding in for one specific job. If your company is a

Richard Evans

specialist in one area, you know you will need more specialists in your team. It is worth investing in video marketing for defined job roles, as they will feature again and again in the future.

As with much of your employer branding, it is about getting the word out to make sure that your video marketing hits as many devices as possible. This enables you to attract the right people to your business. Recruitment will be the most important issue for businesses in the next 20 years, and it is important to start now. To get the right exposure you will need to get your videos on your careers website because that should be developed as the place to visit for anyone looking for work in your industry. In addition to this, it is wise to set up a YouTube account that can house all of the video marketing that your company produces. This will gain you an audience and you can point this audience back to your careers website for further information. Social media shares will also help to raise the profile of your videos and thus raise the profile of the recruitment opportunities you have.

The video makes a connection with your audience in a way that no other content can, until you are face-to-face with a potential employee in an interview situation. It would be very time consuming to speak to everyone in your industry personally; a marketing video for your employer brand is a great alternative. Seeing real people in the video creates connections for the viewer; if you're looking for the top Millennial talent, take that connection to the next level and feature a Millennial in the video. This strengthens your employer brand in the eyes of the Millennial viewer and gives you a much better chance of attracting the type of employee you want to take your business forward.

A great marketing video for your employer brand or a particular vacancy will shout out to the relevant people. If it is done well then it will attract more candidates with better skills and make your recruitment job easier. The Millennial talent wants to work for a company that embraces technology and knows how to use it. If you do this well, you will be able to attract and retain the top Millennial talent.

The importance of SEO

In the recruitment game, the ability to be seen is crucial.

Nobody applies for a job they can't see, and the company that is invisible stays that way. There are many ways of getting your name out there and making sure that potential candidates can find the jobs that you advertise within your sector. In the past this may have been keeping a presence at recruitment fairs or with universities. In the modern age, the power of Search Engine Optimisation is huge. Search Engine Optimisation (or SEO) is the way that your internet content is ranked by search engines such as Google, Bing and Yahoo.

SEO can be a minefield without a well-defined strategy and an experienced SEO Consultant helping out. Google is constantly changes it's algorithms and the way that they rank pages. In the past, it was possible to manipulate these algorithms to ensure that your site ranked well, but this isn't the case anymore. Fresh and relevant content is very much king nowadays.

If you have the right words in the right places then you will increase your rankings and your web content is much more easily found by internet users. For instance, if you regularly recruit for web designers then you will be more likely to get candidates if your job advert appears at the top of a Google search for 'web designer jobs' than if you appear on page 7.

With this in mind, we will take a look at the importance of SEO and what you can do to make sure you make the best of this to attract and retain the top Millennial talent. This is not a part of your business that you can leave to chance. You must have a thought-out and developed strategy to get your website seen and to attract the right people. Having SEO at the forefront of your marketing mind will mean that you succeed in attracting more people to your careers website and fill the vacancies you have in less time with less Expenditure.

You need to make sure that you understand what SEO does to be able to understand what you need to do to make SEO work for you. The search results in which you want to perform well are the searches that the end user will key into their browser when they start the process of trying to find employment. If you company is a manufacturer in Bedford then there is a probability that the end user that you want to attract will search for 'manufacturing jobs in Bedford' when looking for their next job role. This is where you need to focus your content to get as high up the search engine rankings as possible. If you do not have the words 'manufacturing jobs in Bedford' in your careers website you will not naturally appear in the search, so you will not get clicks through to your website and will more than likely have to find another way of attracting the right candidates to your company. This often means more expense and more time. We have looked at the importance of your careers website and the importance of building a pool of talent for your future vacancies. The way to attract people to your company or your talent pool is to allow them to find you. Simple changes to the content on your website can help make that happen.

Make sure that you include the right keywords in your content, and make sure that they feature prominently. Do not put them in every sentence because the bots at the search engines will see this as spam and exclude you from their Results!

The keywords that drive your movement up the search engine ranking are those that mean the most to your company and your potential new employees. The more niche you make these terms (whilst still maintaining the

relevance) then the better and more relevant you will find the results. If you want to attract a specific type of applicant then you need a specific set of keywords that will put you top of that applicant's search.

Google states that 88% of job candidates start their job search on Google. This is a massive pool of potential new recruits for you to tap into. If you speak to your existing team about how they would search for their own job on Google, you can begin to build a picture of where you need to be. If your search terms are unique and still relevant to your potential applicants then you will help yourself get yourself to the front of the SEO queue when it comes to attracting the right Millennial talent to your business to take what you have to the next level. The specific terms that your potential next employee uses to begin their search for a new job are where you need to begin your search for the next employee.

Millennials know how to use technology to get the results they need as quickly as they can. They want to put as little effort as possible into finding the right answers so Google searches will be an easy way to establish the next step in their job hunt. You have to be there as they click through to the results to stand a chance of being part of that job hunt. When a Millennial sees you on the first page they will see that you have a good online presence, you are serious about finding the right people and that you could be the company for them. To meet the Millennial on their own terms and be found in the place that they search first gives you a very good chance of being the employer of choice.

A great way to get your website to carry the right SEO keywords to attract the right quality applicants is to make sure that you carry detailed job descriptions on your website. The job descriptions will quite naturally contain a lot of the right words to get your careers website moving up the search engine rankings for the roles you want to fill, either now or in the future. Make sure that your job descriptions are rich in content and talk about the key skills and experience you require because it is these skills and this experience that will tick the right SEO boxes for your potential applicants.

SEO is driven by quality and relevant content and everything that you include on your careers website should take this into account. Think about the impact of every phrase you use on this part of your website because every phrase increases or decreases your visibility. This is vitally important to your content marketing, your employer brand and your recruitment efforts.

You can work with the search engines such as Google to pay for clicks (which we will cover later) when it comes to looking for the talent you require for the next vacancy your company has. If you haven't got all the SEO work completed to appear naturally in the higher sections of the search engine results, you can pay to move up the rankings. You only pay when someone clicks through the link and you can set a limit for how much you want to spend.

This can be a good strategy if you need to fill a vacancy quickly but in the long run it is more effective to increase your SEO rankings to get you up the ranking and appearing in your own right.

The key focus for your business over the next 20 years is to look for the best talent. Millennial talent will be the major force in this work environment and you need to concentrate your efforts on finding the best way to engage that talent through your marketing. The importance of search engine optimisation cannot be underestimated. It can make the difference between being found or not. If you are found then you fill your vacancies at little extra cost and with ease. If you are not found, you will have to spend so much more time, effort and money to fill your vacancies.

Google Adwords and pay-per-click

There may be times when you want to ramp up your recruitment efforts. It is a great thing to be able to build an employer brand over time, with your content marketing and pool of applicants working away in the background to fulfil future vacancies. But sometimes you may want a quicker solution and feel that paying for results is the right way to go.

Per-per-click (or PPC) is a great way of spending your budget effectively, as you only pay for those that click through your adverts – as you would expect from the title. The more traditional online job boards require you to pay a fee to advertise your vacancy. This fee is payable upfront (and is usually a large fee) for the privilege of advertising your vacancy on their site, whether it gets you one applicant or several hundred. Your advert may be seen and responded to, or you may find that it gets lost on the site. Sometimes you may just have bad timing with when it is posted and be overshadowed by another opportunity. You may get lucky and find that it gains some traction and you get a lot of interest. PPC means that you only pay the advertiser when someone looks at your advert and decides that it is interesting enough for them to click on to. In this case, you pay for what you get.

There are some great benefits to pay-per-click advertising in recruitment.

You only pay when someone clicks through the advert to your careers site

The benefit here is that the people likely to click through will be people who are interested in your vacancy. It means that your advert will only cost you money when someone with an interest, and most likely a relevant skill set, clicks on the link in the advert. You don't pay the traditional job boards the big money to sit there regardless of interest. You pay for the traffic you receive. This method also gives you immediate feedback on whether the advert is working – if you are not getting clicks, you need to make some changes. It is a great way to seek Millennial talent because you will find them online.

You can set how much you want to spend

Paying upfront for exposure on a job board website can become an expensive way to fill your vacancies. You can set the maximum amount you want to spend per day with PPC, so you know that you are getting to the right people and that you have complete control of what you are spending. It means that you can make the advert be what you want it to be – not what the recruitment board website tells you it has to be.

It keeps control of your applicants

Because you set up the link that your applicants follow, you can set up where that link goes to. Job boards will get the applicants to register with them, meaning that they keep all the details that you may want to keep on file for future use. With PPC, you will direct potential applicants to your own careers website, with all the content we have previously discussed. They then see all the engaging content on your website. They become advocates of what you do and are much more likely to apply. All of the content here belongs to you. There is no third-party content, adverts or rival vacancies.

You get measurable results

The results with the recruitment boards are measurable by the boards themselves. They know who they have sent where, what the conversion rate is and how effective they have been. But you want this measurement to be in your hands. PPC gives you the ability to measure how effective your campaign has been. It allows you to see if any changes you make are more or less effective and you can track the way your budget has been spent. Business is about control, especially control of cost, and PPC gives you the ability to gain control over your recruitment efforts in a way that recruitment board websites don't.

PPC works best when your adverts do everything you want them to do. This might sound obvious, but you need to consider what will make a good advert and give you the rate of interest that you require. There are several ways to make sure that your PPC campaign is working at its best. You have to remember certain principles.

Relevance is the absolute key. Your adverts need to find the right audience, so you need to use the right words. An advert that is not relevant to the audience will be ignored, or clicked in error. This goes into the area of keywords and you need to make sure that you have the relevant words that will get your advert seen in all the right places. The job role you are advertising, the industry you are working in and the location of the role are all keywords to feature in the advert so you find the right people.

Working with mobile sites is a larger consideration all of the time. Your Millennial talent will be spending a lot of their time on their smartphone or tablet, so you need to make sure that your advert works on mobile as well. Check out the advert before you make it live to see that it can be easily viewed by your potential audience. The landing page that the applicant clicks through to should be optimised as well. This will be your careers site, so make sure that it works well on smartphones to give the best experience.

You will need to ensure that your adverts perform the way you want them to. If you are running more than one advert this can be a great way to see how effective each advert is. You can check one against the other to see if you need to make any amendments, or whether you need to change them completely. The words that you use will determine the number of people the advert is visible to. You may find that more potential applicants see one set of words than another. Use this information to make your adverts as valuable to your business as possible.

Make sure that your advert has a call to action. This is one of the most important principles of all marketing because without a call to action, your reader won't know what to do next. In PPC the call to action will usually be to click a link through to your careers website, but make sure that it is a relevant link that inspires potential new recruits to move their interest to the next level.

The PPC providers such as Google Adwords will have lots of information on how to make the most effective advertising campaign to fill your job vacancy and attract the best in Millennial talent. Research shows that the early part of the working week is the time when most candidates search and apply for new job roles. Ensure that you have factored this in and that your adverts are running at the right times so that they gain the right audience.

PPC allows you to define the keywords that you do not want to be included. These are known as negative keywords. If you make sure that your negative keywords work for you then you will find a better quality of interest from your adverts and less waste of your budget. If you are looking specifically for one role then you can exclude other similar roles with similar descriptions so you don't get irrelevant clicks that cost you money.

Google Analytics

Once your careers website is set up and loaded with quality, engaging content to attract the best Millennial talent, you will want to know how that website is performing. It is not just a case of seeing how many applicants it provides you. When you use Google Analytics you can see much more detail about your website, such as traffic, where the traffic lives, which links are sending people to your website and which pages are the most popular. All of this information is vital for making a website the best it can be. Once you can see where your visitors come from, how they got to you and what they do when they arrive, you can start to use this information to build a faster, stronger website that will give you even better results.

Installing Google Analytics is easy with even the most basic knowledge of how a website is put together. With your Google account you can search for Google Analytics and enter your website address. On completion of the required information Google will give you a tracking ID code to feature in the code of every page of your website so that each can be tracked. Once done, you will be able to follow the information that Google Analytics produces to see the success rates of each page of website. The data is easy to understand and can be interrogated in different ways.

For the recruiter, you will need to make sure that, along with the other parts of your company website, the careers website has got the Google Analytics tracking ID code added. It then gives you the data you need to see the big picture. There are many terms that are used in Analytics that you may or may not be familiar with. It is useful to understand them from the outset, so here is a short guide to what they mean and what they do for your recruitment business.

Audience Overview gives you stats on the traffic that has visited your site. It breaks things down into users, number of sessions on your site and duration of stay. You can see the effectiveness of your content from the amount of time visitors are spending on your site. The longer they are there, the more engaging you can consider your content. One really useful feature of the Audience Overview section is the **Bounce Rate** statistic. This shows the number of people that left the site after only visiting one page. If you have a lower bounce rate, your candidates are doing more than just looking at a particular job – they are staying and having a look around. This is the sign of a serious candidate.

The most important thing to consider when looking through Google Analytics is what success looks like. It is all very well having facts and figures at your fingertips at all times of the day and night, but they mean nothing unless you know what you are looking for. This may be slightly different for each recruiter; the best way to approach this is to set out what you want to get from your website. The basic equation is that you want to get traffic that joins your talent pool or applies for your jobs. But there are steps along the way to achieving that. Your analysis of the figures in front of you can help you to fully understand what is going on and how you can improve it.

For example, the figures might show that you get a lot of people starting to fill out your application form and then not completing it. From here, you can set the target of getting your application form completion rate to a much higher level. The next step would be to read through the form and see how you can make it easier to understand or shorter to complete. Google Analytics has just given you extra applicants for your future job roles with a simple look at the data they provide you.

Take another example. You may find that a low percentage of people who land on your contact page actually follow this through by getting in touch. So you set yourself the goal of increasing the contact rate through this page. From there, the first port of call will be the contact page itself. Does it include enough ways to get in touch? People may prefer to contact you via Twitter or Facebook; they may want to speak to someone directly or prefer email. Google Analytics has again given you priceless information to improve what you do and gain a bigger response from your website. For recruiters this is crucial. It is much easier to have a big pool of applicants and then assess these and shortlist them than to have an insufficient number of applicants and have to start again. Google Analytics can get you to this level by making everything you do on your careers website as efficient and productive as possible. In fact, when you get up and running with Google Analytics you can set these goals up through the website and measure these specific areas of your website performance. But the key to all of this is to identify the areas that may be letting you down when you check out the reports on Google Analytics.

As with all other forms of recruitment online, your careers website is at its most effective when it is bringing you traffic that is relevant. It is all well and good to have huge viewing figures in New Zealand, but if you only have vacancies in Manchester then it is unlikely that you will get the results you desire when it comes to attracting and retaining the top Millennial talent. Google Analytics gives you the opportunity to look at this area of your recruitment efforts so you can totally see how you are doing here. The real power of Google Analytics is that you can cross-reference the location data with other fields. The UK is not a massive country so it is not beyond the realms of possibility that people might consider relocating. If Analytics tells you that you get a great response in Newcastle but not in Liverpool then you may want to concentrate more on potential new recruits from the North East. You can look at this data in more than one way. You could decide that Newcastle might just be the best place for you to recruit, or you could consider how to change the language you use to appeal to the potential applicants from Liverpool.

Google Analytics gives you the power to see what is working on your careers website, and what is not. From there you can make the necessary changes and tweaks to make it the most powerful tool your employer brand owns. Make sure that you get this added to your careers website and use the data you can access to attract and retain the top Millennial talent as you look to develop your team.

Remarketing

We've all experienced remarketing: you visit a website and, as if by magic, there are adverts on there for something else you've looked at recently – maybe that book on Amazon or the tickets to the match that you were researching. Remarketing is a common strategy and has quite remarkable results. It has been said to help recover up to 96% of the people who visited your site and did not take any action. This is a huge number so remarketing is something that just can't be ignored as a way of attracting and retaining the top Millennial talent. If you miss someone the first time they're on your website, a gentle reminder can help you to attract them the second time they see something from you. This heightens that continual theme of making sure that your marketing and branding is consistent. If you are to use remarketing effectively, the end user needs to be able to quickly make that connection between the remarketing they are seeing and your careers website that they have previously visited. But there is more to it than this, so we will take a look at remarketing and how it can really help you with your recruitment.

Normal internet advertising can be a little hit-and-miss, as you put your adverts on sites that you think and hope will help you, and see what happens. It is only targeted in certain ways but any users that visit the site will see your ad. Some will be relevant, some not. By using cookies, your website can store data on the end user's computer. This means that you can show them adverts on another website that are specifically aimed at that single user. Many of your visitors will have looked at your site and may be considering their next course of action with regards to you and your company. But if they leave your website to make this decision, you have a high chance of losing them forever. Remarketing gives them a further nudge and keeps you in their mind.

Setting it up

This is done through your Google Adwords account. You can alter the exact way in which people receive your remarketing, so that they see your advert if they visit at all, or only if they visit a particu-

lar page, or other criteria that you set. This means that you can cus-
tomise the recipient of your advert. It makes targeting much more
specific and makes the whole process more efficient. You can set
different adverts for different target groups to ensure that your remarketing is as effective as possible. You know that your average
Millennial will spend a lot of time on the internet so they will see
your advert on the next relevant website they click on. It raises the
chance of them re-visiting your careers website and taking action
this time.

Think about your audience

You want your adverts to go to the right people. If you them set up
to be seen by everyone your conversion rate may still be a low figure. A great way to get the right people back to the most relevant
parts of your website is to set up adverts for people who visited a
certain page. If you set it up to appear to all of those that looked at
your subscriber page but took no action, you can target new subscribers to push your talent pool forward and enhance the
perception of your employer brand. If you set up an advert to appear to all of those that started but did not complete a job
application on your website, then you will be getting a second
chance at attracting these applicants. The way in which you strate-
gise your adverts makes a huge difference to how effective they are.
You can also set other parameters, and each needs to be considered
carefully. For example, the amount of time that you store a cookie
on the end user's device is a really important factor. If it is an advert for a specific job vacancy you will want this to be set for a
short period of time because this is when it is relevant. A remarketing advert for your subscriber page will be relevant for a longer
period of time. As with much of the advice in this book, your mar-

keting efforts are about generating relevant website traffic, not just getting numbers for the sake of it.

Your adverts

In order for your adverts to be most effective they need to create a connection with the viewer. The point of the advert is to generate quality clicks back to your website, so consider the elements that make up a good remarketing advert. The ultimate key is the call to action. A strong call to action gives the reader a compelling reason to return to your website and complete the action that they considered on the first visit. Make sure the button to click back to your website is clear and prominent so there is less chance of it being missed. As we know, consistency of branding is vital in remarketing. Make sure your reader knows it's you. You also need to think about where this advert will be seen and subsequently how it will be formatted. Not all sites will format your advert in the same way so you need to make sure it is as adaptable as possible and looks consistently good in all formats.

To make the most of the potential of your adverts you need to check on the data that Google produces to ensure that they are working as well as you want them to. As with all forms of advertising you want to know the success rate to see that you are investing wisely. A great way to do this is to try out different adverts and see what the results are. If one style or type of advert is performing particularly well try to replicate that in your other adverts.

Making it more effective

Your remarketing adverts will work best when you think carefully about what you want to achieve. If your visitors take an action, they are more likely to take another action soon after. For example, if someone signs up as a subscriber with you, they will be likely to follow you on social media if your remarketing adverts prompt them to. This is a great way of leveraging one user action to encourage another. By multiplying your presence in their life, you will be far more likely to attract and retain the Millennial talent that your business is looking for. If you are a part of their online life inasmuch as you feature in their Facebook timeline, they see your tweets and you send them a weekly email, you are more established in their psyche as the employer of choice. This makes recruitment so much easier because you have already converted the Millennial to someone who wants to work with you. All you then need is to find them the right job with your company. It is a case of growing your network to make your recruitment tasks easier now and in the future.

SOCIAL MARKETING

We have looked at recruitment in many ways and forms in this book, and the conclusion that can be drawn is that traditional recruitment is expensive and time-consuming. The rise of the internet and social media means that there are channels out there that are potentially open to you that cost nothing but a little of your time. An added benefit is that the Millennials that you are trying to recruit are high users of social media and you will be able to find them in the places where they actually hang out.

Social media is a great medium to use when supplementing your recruitment efforts because of the lack of cost. Of course, you can pay more to have your posts advertised in a Facebook sidebar or a Twitter featured post, but the essence of social media is that it is free to use. This doesn't mean that you should overuse social media, but quality postings that enhance the perception of your employer brand are hugely positive. This is where an interlinked approach makes real sense to your business, your recruitment and your employer brand. Every part of what you do should offer the same message. The reader needs to know that the 'you' they meet on Facebook is the same as the 'you' they meet on Twitter, on LinkedIn and on your careers website. This is crucial to developing your employer brand and having positive conversations with more people every day. The lack of real cost for social media engagement is a major plus factor. You can take your content from your employer-branded careers website and have it posted on social media to grow your brand. One thing that is important here is that every piece of employer marketing points back at something else. There is the ability on Facebook and Twitter to show your website and include a call to action. Make sure that you make use of these features and show your social media followers the way to find your website. The careers website itself needs to let people know how to follow you on social media. This is a virtuous circle where everything you do references something else. If you can get potential future employees engaging with you on your careers website and all of your social media accounts then you have a much better chance of reaching them with any vacancies you have.

Another advantage of social media is that it is fast. If you spend time building up your following, when it comes to posting about a job advert you can get responses within minutes. The speed at which you can gain a pool of potential applicants is phenomenal. This means that you can go from a new role to a choice of applicants in a matter of only a few hours. The power of this is quite amazing, so you are taking a basic advert in a similar format to the one that you would run in a newspaper and taking the process from a few weeks to a few hours. This has to be a great thing for your recruitment efforts because every minute you go without someone in the vacancy is another minute that something else isn't being done, another minute where a customer may be waiting for a call or another minute where a problem isn't being solved. The vacancy exists because you need someone. The solution is to find the best candidate in the quickest time possible. Social media s a great enabler in this way because it opens up the doors to more people, without direct cost and speeds up the process to boot.

Richard Evans

This is where Millennials come into the equation. The Millennial is adept at social media, so they will be the type of people that will see what you have to say. The next 20 years will be crucial in terms of recruiting the best Millennial talent, so you have to concentrate your recruitment efforts on looking in the right places for the right people.

Social media has been successful in part because of its adoption by the Millennial generation. This is where they hang out. By finding out where your potential next employees hang out and meeting them there on their own terms you can gain a foothold with that group. Your existing team will most likely be on social media and will have friends and family that they are linked to that will fit a similar profile. This is important because you want Millennials to attract Millennials. The generation collaborates well and know how to form teams of talent to solve problems in the workplace for your company and for your customers. To have more Millennials in the workplace as the baby boomer generation retires is a great way to develop your business. After all, a large proportion of your customer base will also be from the Millennial generation.

You want new candidates that are adept at all the technology that can bring benefit to your business. When you market the opportunities your company offers on social media you are communicating with and appealing to a demographic of the population that already uses this technology. Social media is becoming more a part of modern business and you want a team of people that can use it with confidence and manipulate it to bring in results. The Millennial is the prime example of this and you can appeal to their nature by reaching out to them on the social media platforms. They will respond positively to the fact that you have posted details of a job on social media and will be much more likely to apply as it appeals to their sense of getting on with things and getting results by using the easiest method available.

Getting your social media recruitment offering right is a great way to interact with your potential new employees and enhance your employer brand. This means you have a wider reach when it comes to advertising any vacancies that occur and this in turn leads to a better quality of candidate. Everything you do should be about making it easier for you to attract and retain the top Millennial talent. Social media is a fantastic way to get the word out there with little cost but your time. There aren't many ways of operating that you can say cost you nothing. This is why it is such an important way to keep in touch with people. You never know, they might just be your next new recruits.

Paid advertising on social media platforms

The development of social media platforms into something that works for advertisers and made money for the social media companies was a long time coming. When they first launched, there was speculation that these just wouldn't catch the imagination and users would leave social media in droves. How wrong they were. Some have estimated that advertising revenue from social media will reach $11 billion by 2017. This is big business.

To attract the top Millennial talent, you need to be seen in the places that Millennials hang out. To meet them on their own terms in their own backyard, companies need to advertise on the social media platforms where they know Millennials will see those adverts. Banner ads have had their day. The paid search can work really well for a big business that has a lot of money to spend and wants to drive traffic to their website for a certain period of time. It works in generating traffic, and then it is down to the engaging nature of the website to retain those visitors and convert them into customers. But if you don't have money to burn, or can't hone in on the exact keywords you want to use, then you may have to look for a different way to use your budget to find the right applicants. This works whether you are looking for a candidate immediately for an existing vacancy or if you are looking to raise the profile of your employer brand for future vacancies.

You can find more specific adverts on social media because of the amount of information the social media network has gathered on its users. They know where they live; they often know their age and their interests. They often know their employment history. This gives you the advantage that you can have adverts that are aimed at the right people, rather than adverts aimed at the whole population in the hope that the right people might stumble across it. The social media networks have cleverly built up a series of client portfolios that can match a number of searches. You want someone aged 20 to 45, already in an IT job, living within 30 miles of your office? The social media platforms can make sure that your advert goes only to those people that match these criteria. And you only pay for the demographic that matches that profile.

Social networks are a great option for recruiters because of three main reasons. They offer you the ability to target specific readers, the technology works really well on mobile devices and they offer a reliable way of tracking conversions.

The ability to target specific readers

The amount of relevant information that the social media networks gather on their users was a great way for them to build their advertising empires. When you advertise online in general, you may or may not find the readers that you require. It can be the fact that they just happen to see what you are advertising when browsing the internet, or they may just miss you completely. In the business world, every penny counts so you want to know that the money you have set aside for online marketing is actually giving you a return. The beauty of advertising on social media platforms is that they offer the ability to target specific readers. You don't want your advert for a job in Brighton to be clicked on in Borneo or Bora Bora, especially when you are paying for every click that your advert generates. Social media knows where your readers are. Social media has started to look far beyond that as well. It knows how your readers react to paid content. It knows how many people share the content they read, how many click throughs it generates, and any other behaviours when on their platforms.

This gives a reach that you just can't find anywhere else online. The social media platforms can deliver your message to the most relevant, qualified audience available. They give you the people most likely to be interested in the message and the people most likely to respond. When you have a limited budget this is a really efficient way to use your money. You can target your prospects in a few different ways, using the filters social media platforms can apply from the information they have gathered from their users.

There is a tool on Facebook and LinkedIn called 'lookalike targeting', where they provide you with an audience that similar to the users you already have. This helps to grow a similar audience and will give you a better pool of followers for future job adverts because they will be relevant readers that might fit your job profile or share it with someone who does. This allows you to grow your audience quickly but with real people who mean something to your company, rather than paying for followers that might not exist in the real world and that won't engage with your content.

Facebook and Twitter will allow you to upload your own contacts or a list of people and they give you the ability to contact that list through their social media platform. This is known as custom targeting or tailored audiences and you can let the network know the people you want to target, either via email addresses, profiles or phone numbers and they will match these up to their user database and give you that list as the audience for your adverts. This means that you can target a very narrow section of the online community with adverts that you know will be relevant and most probably well-received.

The big social media companies offer 'interest targeting', where you can find users by the interest they list on the networks. This means that for your recruitment efforts you can see people that work in your industry. When we looked at becoming a key business of influence, we looked at how becoming a voice and an authority in your own industry is a positive step to gaining influence and filling job vacancies in less time with less cost. If you can target people that are already working in your industry this gives you a leap forward in two areas. First, you will be able to fill current vacancies much more quickly with an advert because you know it will be seen by those that work in a similar role in your industry. Secondly, you develop followers in your own industry as you start to develop

134

your influence and create a pool of talent that will be ready to apply for any future vacancies that arise.

Technology on mobile devices

Social media has become as big as it is in part because of the massive use of mobile devices. You can check your social media updates on the move just about anywhere now. Your adverts will reach the right audience wherever they are in the world, so you don't have to wait for the audience to be sat at a desktop to read what you want to show them. It is said that Facebook and Twitter make the majority of their advertising income from mobile advertising, so this backs up the fact that these are read by users and they work for organisations. This will only get bigger because the use of smartphones is on an upward trend, not a downward one.

You have to think about the best way to spend the budget you have to advertise when recruiting, so using a method that you know can reach your target audience (especially the audience of Millennials that are high users of social media) makes absolute sense from all angles.

A reliable way of tracking conversions

Business is all about measuring the effectiveness of the money that you spend. Most recruitment departments are beholden to the wider organisation in terms of gaining and spending a budget. You need to spend that money effectively and prove the effectiveness of that expenditure. Social media platforms offer a reporting system that allows you to track your conversions and see the value you get from the adverts that you place with them.

Advert on social media always include a call to action. This means that the end user is persuaded to click a link, complete a registration or to get in touch. When these requests are compelling enough, they generate followers, new users and buyers. It transforms simple marketing into an exercise to drive your recruitment efforts forward. By getting this right you will be able to get a much higher conversion rate than with any other form of advertising either online or offline. The social networks give you the ability to add a tracker to your adverts so you can see the impact they are having and the results they are getting.

Every penny counts, so to be able to follow the progress of your adverts and report this progress back is an invaluable tool when it comes to spending your company's money wisely. There is so much to get right here that you will want the latest facts and figures at your fingertips before you propose the next set of spending. Recruitment is a part of the business that could draw huge resources if you wanted to cover every base. But by spending the right amounts in the right places you can get a grip of the costs and get the best return on that investment.

Paid advertising on social media can be a great way to fill vacancies quickly or to grow your employer brand. When these paid adverts are used in the right way, you can get a great return on the money you spend, reach a more precise audience and check up on how well the money has been spent.

Promote and engage on Facebook

There are many ways to get your recruitment messages out there, whether to enhance your employer brand, develop your talent pool or generate quality applicants for the latest vacancy. But there are not many sources that can give you access to over a billion users. Facebook has 1.5 billion users, according to statista.com. The power of Facebook is evident for all areas of your business but for recruitment it can be an absolutely vital way to engage the people that you want to work for you in the future. This is especially relevant for attracting and retaining the top Millennial talent because the average Millennial is a high user of social media sites such as Facebook.

The first step on this road is to have a company Facebook page to get your presence seen on the network. The content that is related to your recruitment can link straight back to your careers website so that you capture users immediately. You then start to gain an audience on Facebook for the employer brand that you are developing all the time. But the content that you include on your Facebook page must be as relevant and engaging as the content you provide in all other areas of your recruitment efforts. You will gain followers, likes and shares through great content on your Facebook page and this can be seen by potential candidates. It means that you gain access to a new market of people that could be the next new recruit for your company and all for the cost of nothing but some of your time.

The page needs to do certain things for your company. First, it needs to have the same formatting, logos and message as all of your other recruitment advertising. A consistent message is key to ensuring that your readers know who you are and what you do. One area where you can make this happen effectively is in your company description at the top of your profile. It should include your logo, and be clear and concise when it comes to explaining who you are and what you are doing on Facebook.

You need to consider the content you will include and how this will interact with and engage your potential new recruits. A great image can do much more than paint a thousand words. If the image is relevant and engaging it will gear up your audience to read through, like and share the information you put with it. This is the way you grow your audience and get your name out there. When you are looking for new recruits one great way to show what a great place your company is to work is to show the working environment. You should be proud enough to show Facebook followers (and don't forget that these may include people who are qualified to work in your company) the location that you work in and the things that make it interesting. This will engage readers and attract similar people. If you have a high proportion of Millennial talent in your organisation already, the work environment they create is likely to attract more Millennial talent in the future. To go alongside this you can feature the people who work there. A photo with a short caption will really create the image of the vibrant and happy team that works in your company. This is a fantastic way to attract new recruits because they can see the team dynamic.

The crossover between your careers website and your Facebook page will give you the opportunity to feature some of the other work you have been doing as a recruiter and to develop your employer brand. We have looked into video marketing and how useful this can be in terms of things like engaging potential candidates and increasing your search ranking. Including this video content on Facebook is a great idea because it further engages your audience. Your followers will want to see diverse posts from you. Video content is another way of showing that you are an employer that is able to operate across a broad spectrum of media.

This content can be enhanced by keeping your audience up to date with any other office news, such as charity events, new employees, employer or employee awards and events in your industry. The more complete you make the timeline of your Facebook feed, the more likely you are to find the right people. This also applies to the feeds of others in your industry. As you start to use Facebook as a networking tool, you will find other companies similar to yourself, other recruiters or people who are influencers in your industry. By liking them (and asking for a reciprocal like back) and writing interesting and relevant comments on their timeline, you will start to widen your sphere of influence. To become a respected voice in your industry you need to get your message out there and by using Facebook to reach more people you increase the visibility of your brand.

Once you are using your company Facebook page to post relevant and interesting information about your company's recruitment efforts then you will start to see the benefits. But this is not the be all and end all of Facebook recruitment. Your posts will be commented on, liked and shared. You will get user requests and people will ask all sorts of questions of you. So you need to make sure that you can manage the Facebook page and give someone the task and time to stay on top of it. You want your content to be engaging. But engaging content will draw comments and questions. You need to respond to those questions in a timely and professional manner. The benefits of a great Facebook page will be undone if you can't respond to your users and manage their expectations of what service the page will provide. If you include the opening times of your business on the description then people will know whether their query will be responded to at any time or only in office hours. This makes sure that you protect your employer brand, because someone who expects a response within 2 hours and has to wait 2 days will be unlikely to apply for any positions that you advertise.

The brand that you build on Facebook needs to be as credible as the brand you are building elsewhere. It will take time to build up the content that will attract followers that may include your next candidates. But because of the reach that Facebook can give you and the low cost to set it up, it is a website that every company should have a presence on. When you do it right, your Facebook presence becomes something that drives quality traffic to your careers website to fill any potential vacancies that you have now or in the future.

Promote and engage on Twitter

The use of social media to fill job vacancies or to grow your employer brand can be a daunting one, especially to the uninitiated. But when the market that you should be aiming at (the Millennial generation) spends a lot of time on social media then you need to grow your presence there. I have reiterated many times that you need to learn where your audience hangs out and hang out there too, so Twitter is an absolute must for the recruiter that wants to attract the top Millennial talent.

Twitter is a really useful tool to engage the right people and direct them to everything else that you offer. Each time you post something (a tweet) you are limited to a maximum of 140 characters. So you will not be able to give chapter and verse on what you do or what you have to offer, but you will be able to prompt people to take a further look at what you do and follow the links that you add to the tweet. The traffic should be directed to your careers website because this is where you have assembled your killer content that will attract candidates. There are some great tips for getting started on Twitter and making the most of your Twitter account for all your recruiting needs. Remember that the beauty of Twitter is the fact that it is free to use and you can open up new audiences that you may not have been able to access otherwise.

The first decision you have to make is how to set up your Twitter account. You have a few decisions to make here and they can impact on how you are received and followed in the future. You have to decide whether you want this to be a corporate account (basically an extension of everything else you do) or a personal account as yourself. Twitter is quite a relaxed medium so either may work for you; it just depends on what you want from it. To add to this, you need your profile information, such as contact details, website links, images and a basic description of who you are and what you do. This description is also limited to 140 characters so you need to be straight to the point. Make sure that everything you put together here shows a consistent message from wherever else you have exposure. It needs to have a similar feel to your careers website, your Facebook presence and anywhere else you reside on the internet. Consistency means that those who find you will know that it is the same you that they can see elsewhere. You want people to see what you have to offer and feel as though you are someone they can follow so make sure that you fill in all the fields, add all the relevant images and make your presence felt.

The first step after this is to tweet. This is subject to the 140 char-acter limit, but aside from this, anything goes. You will have content already on your careers website, so it can be a good idea to give short descriptions and provide links to your careers website. Any blogs that you put together as part of your content marketing are also a great idea to feature on Twitter because you will find relevant followers by posting what you do, and what you already have produced. The people who will want to follow you will be interested in the same things that you are. If you work in IT and post about IT subjects then you will be found and followed by those with an interest in IT as well. This is where hashtags come into play. A hashtag (#) is a tool that Twitter uses to establish trends and allow people to search for common interests. If you are hiring, a hashtag of #hiring or #newjob or something similar will allow you to attract those that use that hashtag to search. There are many websites that will give you the top hashtags in your field or area so you will be able to use these to attract the right people.

Although tweeting on a regular basis and using the right hashtags will attract followers for your Twitter profile, there are other ways of attracting people to increase your following. If you follow others then there is often a good chance that they will follow you. But some followers are more valued than others. It may be great to have 20,000 Twitter followers but if they are not relevant to you or your industry then they won't make potential new recruits. You can gain followers in the right places by following those that mean something to you. Start with members of your existing team because these people will also know others in your industry and you can grow your sphere of influence quickly this way. You will also want to follow any leading lights in your industry and from there start to look at the people that follow them.

Grow your following by looking in the right places for relevant followers that may be able to help you gain a wider influence or may be future candidates for job vacancies. To have thousands of followers no matter what is a vanity project. To have relevant followers that may turn your social media efforts in job applications means that you are doing the right things.

You can also increase your influence by re-tweeting the posts of others. If you see something particularly relevant or interesting that relates to your industry or something in the news that affects what you do, by re-tweeting what someone else has said or linked to then you can grow your own following by showing that you are in touch with what is going on. The recruiter that uses Twitter to meet others and converse with them will be the recruiter that doesn't look as though they are only in it for the money. Twitter is a community, and if you take part in that community and use the principles of give and take, you are much more likely to develop a relevant and vibrant following.

Twitter gives you the ability to keep in touch with your customers and potential candidates but it also allows them to keep in touch with you. Your Twitter account is something that has to be monitored and actively managed because you must respond quickly to any questions or suggestions. If you advertise a job vacancy on Twitter and a potential applicant asks you a question there you will need to answer that question quickly. The Millennial generation have grown up to expect quick answers to any questions they ask.

Twitter can be a great tool to enhance your recruitment efforts if it is used correctly. When you have a great profile that complements what you do elsewhere, engaging content and links back to your careers website then you will have another weapon in your armoury. You need to tweet regularly and make sure that you respond to any questions you get. If you manage to get all of these things right, you will find that Twitter is a great channel to use in your recruitment efforts now and in the future.

Promote and engage on LinkedIn

The power of social networks for any aspect of business is increasing by the day. When you can access a huge number of people from all over the world in an instant, you will be able to reach out to markets, customers and potential employees that your offline advertising just could not reach. But the traditional social networks such as Facebook and Twitter are just that – somewhere that many people hang out socially. They can still be used as a resource for your recruitment needs as we have already seen, but there is a network that gives you the ability to meet fellow professionals. That network is LinkedIn. This is a network that will allow you to grow what you do by linking with fellow professionals in your own industry. This will facilitate many of the other things we have already looked at so far, such as building a pool of talent and developing your employer brand. LinkedIn has some unique features that don't apply to the likes of the other social networks, so let's take a look at how you can make it work for your recruitment.

LinkedIn works differently to other networks because the links that are created between people are as important as the people themselves. For instance, if you look for a candidate from a particular background, the people that they are linked to will more than likely have a similar background. It is not just your contacts that may be your next new recruit, but their contacts as well. If you are look-ing to fill a specific role, you should look first at the people you are directly connected to. Once you have looked through this list and identified a small number of ideal candidates, you can take the next step. From there you will want to look at the connections that these candidates have. People on LinkedIn tend to cluster by indus-try, so the ideal candidates will more than likely generate even more great candidates for you, because they will be connected to others in the same industry, with the same skills and the same expe-rience. The power of LinkedIn is that you can suddenly transform a list of a few candidates into something that resembles a pool of talent by using the network in the right way. The idea is then to dig a little deeper into this longer list of candidates to whittle them down into something that will be useful to you in terms of a con-tact list.

All of this means that rather than using LinkedIn to type in a cer-tain job role and look at people who already do that job, you are looking at the connections formed and how this dynamic may fit your company. If you search day after day with the same search term then you will find the same result day after day. If you look at the connections that people have made and continue to make, you will find a new set of people every time you search. Your ideal can-didates for current and future vacancies will be more likely found this way.

LinkedIn gives you the ability to see much more information than other social networks. You can see a person's employment history, so you can see what roles they have previously filled and how this may relate to the role you have vacant. You can see their comments or posts and this builds a picture of the type of candidate they are likely to be. Remember that we began by looking at the characteristics a Millennial will likely have. They will want to make a difference, they will want to feel valued and they will want to move up the ladder quickly. It's this type of dynamic and go-getting employee that you can use LinkedIn to find when looking to fill your next vacancy.

There are no two ways about it: your competitors have some employees that you'd rather worked for you. I'm not, of course, suggesting that you go through a headhunting or poaching process and strip your rival's team from under them. But the way in which LinkedIn is structured means that you have a great way of starting a search for new recruits for a current vacancy or to increase your pool of applicants in the future. From the main profile of a company page on LinkedIn, you will find a list of those who work for them. When you pull down this list you will be able to see the full names and details of all of those that work there. In addition you can start a process similar to the one above by looking at these people's connections and how they interact with those connections. You will see links between these guys and your current team, and you can again see the work history of your competitor's employees. Use this list wisely; it can give you a great guide to who you'd want to contact for the vacancy you need to be filled.

When this approach is used in conjunction with the sourcing from profile to profile, as above, it grows your candidate list and allows you to filter down by quality in a much more robust way. If you only identify five candidates, you're going to reach out to all five. If you use the power of connectivity that LinkedIn gives you, you could well have a candidate list of 50. From here you can apply further filters and maybe only contact the best 10. Immediately you have been more selective and still got a better, longer list of candidates. Using LinkedIn in the right way means that you open up the field of people you can contact, so you get a better quality of applicant in the immediacy and in the long run.

One of the strongest features of LinkedIn is the way in which they have given users the ability to form and join groups. It means that like-minded people can join together to form a small community within the big community of the entire network. The smaller groups are a great place for you to source potential new recruits because you know that members of a particular group will be working in or interested in a certain industry or area of expertise. For instance, there is an estate agents UK group on LinkedIn; this is full of estate agency professionals that you can mine for your recruitment campaigns. You can use the list of members of a group in a similar way to how you'd use the list of employees for a rival. It will give you a starting point for your search. Again, you will be able to look at their current role, their work experience and their skills to see how close a match they are to your needs. It may be a really big group and you may have to work through it to cut it down to a manageable size, but the results will definitely be worth it. The top Millennial talent will almost definitely have a profile on LinkedIn because they see and understand the value of it. You now know how to harness this value and make it work for you. When recruiting for your next vacancy, you can go on to the free network that LinkedIn gives you access to and look for suitable applicants because you can see how connections work.

Promote and engage on YouTube

The plethora of ways to promote and market your recruitment online can be a little daunting, because there are so many places to look and so many different ways to advertise. It can be best to select a few quality areas that you know have great audience numbers and are established, especially among the Millennial talent that you are looking to attract. YouTube is a fantastic tool for reaching a large and diverse audience to grow your employer brand and for recruiting your next employees. It is established enough that you can create legitimate recruitment content for YouTube and find the right candidates time after time. It is a specialist area, so you need to get it right. Here is a guide to setting up your YouTube account in the right way to attract and retain the top Millennial talent.

You need to register and set up your YouTube channel correctly. As with all of the marketing areas we have looked at, it is imperative that you keep a consistent message here. You want your audience on all platforms to understand that it is your company and that the marketing message goes together. Your YouTube channel will filter viewers into your careers website so you want this traffic to know that the site they land on is run by the same people as the YouTube channel. The logos, the colour scheme and the wording must mirror those that you use in all the places you have an online presence. You need to choose your icon and art for your YouTube account; make sure that these show who your company is and also show why people should continue to engage with you. This is all about creating an impact, enticing your audience to stay and feeding them through to your careers website to join your talent pool or apply for specific jobs. You need to think about how the icon and art will be seen on all formats – from PCs to laptops, from smartphones to tablets. View your YouTube channel on all formats to make sure that it does what you want it to do.

The next step is to set up a trailer for your channel. Your YouTube channel will really serve two purposes – to enhance the promotion of your employer brand and to recruit candidates for your business. So the trailer will need to cover both these bases in an entertaining and informative way. If you are unsure how to do this, take a look at some of the other brands on YouTube and how they put their trailer together. You will see good and bad examples that will help to inform you on where you want to go with this. This trailer will be seen by non-subscribers when they first visit your channel so you need to make it engaging and persuasive. You want to turn the first-time viewer into a long-term fan. Once you have your channel set up and your trailer in good shape, the next step is to add relevant links. If people like your YouTube channel, they should be encouraged to follow you on Twitter, like you on Facebook and visit your careers website. It is by interlinking all the media you utilise that you can increase your exposure and get a following to increase the influence you have in your industry. The key business of influence will, as we know, attract more applications than other companies and get better quality applicants in a shorter space of time with less cost.

Once you have a channel set up, the way to get recruiting is to up-load videos. There are certain ways of making sure that the content you upload is interesting, shared and followed. You want the viewers to keep watching, return to your channel in the future, share the video with their contacts and click through to your careers website. All this is quite a tall order. But there are a few tricks that can help you along the way. The first 15 seconds of your video are absolutely crucial to the viewer. In this short space of time you need to give them a reason to stay. In that short space of time, you need to build trust or spark curiosity. Because of this, you need to front-load your video with the right information. It's no good having a great ending to the video if the start isn't good enough to get the viewer that far. What you can do is give a teaser of what can be found at the end. If the video is, say, about top tips on how to apply for a job, you can preview the best tip at the start, and then fully reveal it at the end. This way, you get buy-in at the start of the video and are likely to keep the viewer hooked until the end. On this subject, your videos can be as public-service as this. Your viewers won't want to subscribe to a channel that's full of job adverts and information about how great your company is. You need to produce content that the audience finds informative and useful. This grows the audience and retains it. It grows your employer brand because you give them a reason to return.

At the end of each video you need to include a call to action. This may be to view another specific video, to visit your careers website or to follow you on other social media sites. The call to action changes what might be an enjoyable video into something that your viewer acts upon to the benefit of both parties. You need to create and upload content regularly for your subscribers. People follow a YouTube channel because they want to see more. You need to provide them with more. Each time you do, the content needs to be as useful and engaging as the previous time, and it needs to arrive regularly. Creating something that gives ideas, hints and tips to applicants really works. They may not eventually use these ideas to apply for positions with your company, but it increases the chance that they might.

Using YouTube can provide access to a new audience that can massively increase your employer brand and give you a way to find new recruits. However you produce your content, it needs to engage your audience (quickly), and then prompt them to act in a certain way. Millennials will spend a good deal of time on YouTube, as they do on other social media sites. Your presence on YouTube will be noticed by Millennial talent and if you give them something useful then they will give you something in return – their time, their subscription and the spread of your content to their peers. Don't expect overnight success or your videos to go viral, but remember that you don't need either of these things to build a strong employer brand. You need good quality content that is viewed by the relevant people to fill vacancies, whether now or in the future.

Emerging social recruiting platforms

Throughout the book we have looked at the different options available to you when it comes to building an employer brand and recruiting new talent. We have seen that Millennials are big users of social media platforms, and taken a quick tour through how you can get the most out of using Twitter, Facebook and LinkedIn to attract talent. There are other social media platforms that are starting to emerge that you can use to increase the power of your brand and capture the interest of those you may have missed on other networks. These have high numbers of users and are growing all the time, so they are definitely worth investigating for your recruitment. The two that are gaining traction are Instagram and Snapchat. We will take a look at both and how you can make the most of their power and reach.

Instagram

Instagram is big. It currently has around 300 million users, with an average of 70% of those logging in daily. These are active users that spend a good deal of time browsing the site. It is this browsing that you can use to your advantage. As an extension of everything you do on your careers website, you can set up an Instagram profile. It is as easy to do as those on other social networks and is free. The app was initially used to apply filters and other finishing touches to your photos. But Instagram really took off when it became more like the other social networks in terms of being able to like, share and follow other users. This saw it grow massively and the appeal with the Millennial generation is strong.

This is a great tool for enhancing your employer brand because you can use photographs to tell the story of what it's like to work in your company. Instagram can give you the audience to tell this story. Potential employees want to know what it would be like to work for you. You can show behind-the-scenes photos of people doing the interesting and stimulating tasks that your company carries out.. For example, if you manufacture and sell tech products, your Instagram account might be a mix of the cool products you produce along with images of them being made, your team having fun and images of your high-tech facility that produces the products. It is all about creating an image of your company from the front to the back, including the things that non-employees would never usually see – these are the things that potential employees want to know. As with all of your social media marketing it needs to produce an end result. Use the website to enhance your employer brand, but don't forget to include a call to action. This can be to like, share or follow, but can also link to your other social media presence or your careers website. The point of having this presence is to get new recruits; never lose sight of this fact when you are producing the photographs.

The power of Instagram can be multiplied in several other ways depending on the company you are and the industry you operate in. If you are, say, a tech or marketing company that is looking to hire tech or marketing talent, you will probably find more traction on Instagram than others, as your potential candidates are more likely to be a part of the community.

Snapchat

This is another growing platform that can be useful to recruiters because of the sheer number of users, and because it continues to grow and grow. It allows users to upload photos, add video and include text or drawings, and then send them to a chosen list of addressees.

This again taps into the enhancement of your employer brand by connecting with the right people in the places that they already populate. You can connect with Millennials who might not be on the other social networks such as Facebook and Twitter, and because of this you can grow your brand. As always, make sure that you include contact information and a call to action. This is not a vanity project, but a way to get people to interact with your employer brand in a meaningful way that will lead to them taking actions that will benefit your company. It allows you again to tell the story of your company and your people. Encourage your team members to record a quick Snapchat video on your account to show how they feel about working for you. This is a really positive way of getting that message out there. You want the relevant world to see that they'd be motivated and happy to work for your company.

The next step with Snapchat is to use it in a more innovative way for recruitment. If you want to embrace this technology, why not have your recruitment show first on Snapchat? You could send a short message to your Snapchat followers to tell them that something big is happening, and direct them to where they can find more information. This means that if your followers want the information before anyone else, they get that by following you on Snapchat.

Snapchat is a great way of involving people in what you do on a daily basis or at a certain event. If you are holding a recruitment event, a Snapchat update with the permission of those attending is a great way to build excitement and tell the story of what it's like to be a candidate for you and to work for you. Remember when we looked at your email marketing content being useful and usable for your readers? Well, this applies here, too: Snapchat can offer a valuable insight to anyone who wants to work for you, or who is preparing for a similar day themselves. By keeping your content fresh and relevant you will not only grow your followers, but retain the ones you already have, too.

For companies that are really cutting-edge, they could encourage people to answer interview questions or submit super-short job application videos to Snapchat, to get an insight into their new candidates and how they interact with technology.

Both Instagram and Snapchat are fun ways to get your existing team and your potential new recruits involved in your company and the recruitment side of it. This has two effects on your employer brand. In the first instance you immediately make it a more fun place to work because your team will be involved in taking and uploading photographs and interacting on social media. The second factor is that you improve the perception of your employer brand with your followers, because they can see it's a fun place to work. You can do your employer brand a lot of good by using the platforms that are available to you, including the ever-expanding Instagram and Snapchat.

PART 4
LOOKING AHEAD

MEASURE YOUR RESULTS

When it comes to your recruitment you can get a feel for how well you are doing by finding out from people within the business how they feel about the quality of the newest recruits, and how easy they're finding it to fill vacancies. Feelings are a useful gauge, and they should not be ignored, but there is a far more scientific and measurable way of seeing how your recruitment processes are performing. As you seek to attract and retain the top Millennial talent, you need to know exactly what is going on to determine the results of your actions and how to deliver improvements. The whole ethos of what you do should be a continual arc of improvement. You're reading this book because you want to improve your recruitment. We have outlined the areas in which you can look to improve, such as the development of your employer brand, your place as a key business of influence and the use of social media to attract new talent. But all of this means nothing if it doesn't do what it sets out to do. You need to measure your progress. To do this, you need to look at the data available to see how effective and efficient your recruitment efforts are.

The way in which results are measured may differ from business to business and industry to industry, because each company may have a different area of focus. But there are two main measures for any recruitment – cost and success rate. These can be broken down into different factors, so let's take a look at some of the areas that you will want to monitor.

The cost of hiring each new employee

This is the big one. If you have to report your success back up to the senior management of your company, this is the first place they'll look. It is the measure of the total recruitment costs divided by the number of new recruits. The senior management in your company will want to see a downward trend of the cost as you develop alternative (and more efficient) methods of recruitment. By using social media and developing an employer brand, you should see your long term costs reduce and your effectiveness increase. Cost is a major factor in the decision-making of any company, and there will always be an eye on the cost-efficiency of every department within the organisation. When costs get too high in a particular department, it comes under scrutiny and this can be when outsourcing happens. Your job is to deliver an efficient service that costs the company less than the alternatives – but driving down costs while ignoring other factors is not the route to success.

How long it takes to fill a vacancy

If you carry out a great, low-cost recruitment drive, but it takes forever to fill a vacancy, you are not fulfilling your role. The length of time taken to hire goes hand-in-hand with cost to establish the efficiency of your recruitment efforts. When you are looking to recruit and retain the top Millennial talent, you need to act quickly and hang out in the places that Millennials hang out. We know that they are high users of technology and want answers quickly, so if you are taking months to recruit you are probably looking in the wrong places. By driving down the time taken to fill a vacancy, you are keeping colleagues motivated, customers happy and the company as efficient as possible.

Where your applicants come from

The tracking of the source of your applicants (and, further, the tracking of those that are actually hired) is a great way to record the most efficient uses of your resources. Without this, you can't spot trends, maximise the best sources or eliminate those that don't bring you in anything. Your time and budget are valuable resources that need to be protected at all costs. Once you know where your spend is bringing you the right applicants, you know where to spend your time and money. Without this information, you could plough a lot of time into something that doesn't do anything for your employer brand or your recruitment.

How good the applicants are

The quality of the respondents to each new role that you advertise is far more difficult to measure, and will need some subjectivity to produce, but it is a very important measure of how successful your recruitment is. It is all well and good to have hundreds of applicants for every job you advertise, but if there are no applicants of the required quality, this is a key area for improvement. It may be that you looked in all the wrong places, in which case you can re-advertise in more appropriate channels. It could be that your advert did not explain the criteria in enough detail; thus, you should change the job description when you advertise again. The fact that you have measured the quality of the applicant means that you have an insight into where things may have gone wrong (or right) and where to improve (or retain) features for the future.

How new recruits assimilate into the existing team

We know how critical it is to fill a vacancy quickly – yet, equally, it's vital that the vacancy isn't filled with unsuitable new recruits. How these new recruits fit into the existing team and how quickly they get up to speed is a great measure of the suitability of the new hires. If the new recruits don't reach the required standard quickly, they are more of a drain on resources than an asset. The recruitment team will come under scrutiny if they continually produce poor quality hires, even if they are quick and cheap. The flip side of this is to measure the number of new recruits that leave the business quickly. Generally speaking, new recruits are hired with the intention of them staying long term, so every time a new starter leaves within the first 12 months you need to ask the question – why did they leave? If you are hiring unsuitable applicants, this leaver rate will increase.

The simple fact is that you want to see the results of your hard work. When you look at the number of happy new recruits that you have hired, it is easy to be blind to the facts and figures that back up the work you have put in. By looking at cold, hard facts you can see the cost of what you do and where that fits in the whole organisation. Recruitment is as subject to budgetary controls as any other part of a business, so when it is carried out in a more efficient and relevant way, this is noticed. You need to see where to spend your time and money, because there is a finite amount of each. Make sure that you have a grip on everything that you spend on recruitment, and an understanding of how hard that money is working for the business.

ON-BOARDING NEW RECRUITS

On-boarding your new recruits is a really important part of the process because it enables integration and helps to stop those new recruits (who, let's not forget, have cost you a lot to hire) from leaving in the initial period of their employment. n-boarding isreally important to your business and t you need to deliver it effectively in order to get the most out of the relationship between the new recruit and your company. So there are steps that you need to take to ensure that you on-board new recruits effectively.

The initial on-boarding process is the ideal chance to explain the culture of the company and how the new recruit fits in. This should be an extension of everything else that has happened up to this point. The culture of the company should have come through in the employer brand, in the job advert and in the selection process, but this is the chance to make that stick. The best on-boarding is a mixture that considers the technical aspects of the job alongside the emotional aspects of the job. The culture of your organisation should be laid out in all the processes that happen in on-boarding to embed this attitude in your new recruits. The first impressions are the ones that last. Creating the right ones ensures that you don't lose good employees through a lack of efficient integration. The Millennial generation want to work for a company that shares their values. This will have come through in the whole recruitment process, and can be reinforced here.

When a new recruit accepts a role with you, it is easy to sit back and wait for them to serve their notice with another employer, and then give them a few weeks to settle into their new role. This is not the ideal way to keep a new recruit engaged with your organisation or to make them feel valued. The lines of communication should be open throughout this period to ensure that any issues are re-solved and any questions answered. There should be regular contact from the line manager to the new recruit while they are serving their notice period at another employer. This keeps interest levels high, and ensures that they understand how valued they will be when they start with the company. Once they begin their new role, arrange regular meetings to see how they are progressing and if there are any areas that need to be addressed. The quality em-ployer understands that this is a key time in any employment, and that a lack of communication can have a hugely detrimental effect on the new employee. Gathering feedback on the new team mem-ber from other members of the team is another valuable way to see how they are integrating, but make sure that this information is collected in the right way, rather than it becoming gossip. The genuine feedback gathered can have a positive impact on setting the tasks in the on-boarding process that will have the biggest im-pact on the integration of the new team member.

It is useful to divide the on-boarding process between different team members at different times. This gives a fresh perspective on the new recruit from each new existing team member they encoun-ter and allows the new recruit to develop relationships that will be valuable to them in their future at the company. This enables the new employee to see the company from different angles and to ask questions of people from different levels and different departments. The more engaging and different the approach, the more the new recruit will reap from it. This also allows you to gather more feed-back to make the on-boarding process individual to each new employee. In addition, it enables the new starter to see all of the different departments and how they fit together to make the whole company. This again taps into the culture of the organisation and helps the new starter learn who to go to when they need a resolu-tion from a department that isn't their own.

We have all been in a new job; one of the first things that happens is a whirlwind tour of all the people that you will be working with. It goes by in a blur and you remember almost nothing. It is an in-effective way of making an introduction because you never get time to ask a question, remember a name or work out what someone does. A much better solution is to allow a conversation and get your new recruit actually acquainted with the existing team. Break it down into small groups, arrange a coffee break with them and the new starter, and let them have a chat. It breaks the ice, allows personality to come through and enables each side to ask a few questions. Repeat this until the new recruit has had a chance to sit down with the whole team. It shows that you are an employer who thinks about the on-boarding of your valued new team member and establishes better relationships quickly.

On-boarding needs to be as engaging and interesting as possible, because you are still in the early stages of selling your company to your new recruit. To help make this as compelling as possible, you need to make the tasks relevant and varied. Day after day of shad-owing someone else or page after page of reading does nothing for the new recruit and can actually damage their opinion of your company. You have explained in your recruitment process that you are a dynamic and interesting company to work for. From this, you have attracted the top Millennial talent. The next step is to live those values and make the job interesting from day one. The effective on-boarder will have thought about everything that a new recruit needs to know, and put together a plan of how they will learn it and who they will learn it with. So a typical day might be:

- shadowing someone in the same department in the morning
- a coffee break with another department
- taken out for lunch by one of the directors
- a chance to question someone in the operations team after
- a meeting with the line manager to discuss progress and agree actions for the next week

The actual plan will depend on your company, but the fact is that this is a far more interesting and stimulating day than one spent reading the policy and procedure manual. Make sure that your on-boarding process does not put your valuable new recruit off your company.

In all, the on-boarding process is an important part of how you look after the new recruit that you've just spent a lot of time and money attracting to your organisation. You need to make the on-boarding as effective as possible, because this is an investment that you want to protect. When you get it right, you produce employees that add to your employer brand and integrate into their new role effectively and quickly.

START AND END WITH 'WHY?'

Finally, and most importantly of all, let's look at how businesses inspire action....

Businesses should ask why they're following certain paths, should constantly interrogate their own logic and never take their eyes off the prize; they should have a clear plan of what they're doing and why, whether it's developing their employer brand, marketing, social media or on-boarding.

Simon Sinek, author of *Start With Why*, believes that great leaders and businesses inspire others by understanding the 'why' in everything they do.

Sinek's belief is that all great leadership and inspiration starts with the question of **'Why?'**

He explores several people and moments in history. He comes to the conclusion that there must be something special about those who become great leaders and inspire those around them to achieve.

Apple is just one of many big players within technology, and the Wright Brothers were not the only ones who were attempting to give people the gift of flight. So what makes these different to those around them? Sinek believes that those who become inspirational are able to tap into a different vein of thinking to everyone else.

While this idea may sound complex, it is actually pretty simple. Sinek refers to it as the 'golden circle'. This concept is all about doing what you do every day, but knowing *why* you do it. This is also why you should never settle for simply making a profit or lining your pockets. Leaders who inspire have a whole new approach to the 'why?' question that enables them to stand out.

When we consider the 'why?' before we do things, it affects our actions and the methods that we choose to communicate with each other. By changing the way we look at the world from the outside in, our ideas become crystal clear.

Communicating in this manner allows us to distil complex ideas and make them easier to understand. To use the Apple example again, Apple does not present itself as a company that simply makes computers and electronic products. It presents itself as a company that is interested in changing the status quo. A company that pushes the boundaries.

It succeeds because it knows why it is in business in the first place, not just because its products are good. If you don't know why you are doing something, it is next to impossible to get people to follow you. Leaders are not in the business of inspiring people to get what they have; they are in the business of getting people to think in the same manner as they do, to view the world through a different prism.

Richard Evans

In today's crowded marketplace, no one is going to buy into you your company if you do not know why you are in business in the first place.

A great business inspires its employees by working with a sense of purpose and by having the presence of mind to know that people do not follow because they have to.

People follow because they want to. Starting with 'why?' is the best way to get people on board with where you are and, most importantly of all, where you are heading.

Consider your 'why?' when you are developing your communications and promoting your employer brand to your talent community.

ABOUT THE AUTHOR

Richard is the Founder of Bold Identities & Bold Careers, two businesses that share the same goal "to help organisations attract and engage the best talent".

Bold Careers is a boutique recruitment firm that place graduate sales talent into some of the UK's leading ambitious businesses.

Bold Identities are a full service marketing and technology agency that specialise in Employer Branding and Recruitment Technology.

Bold Identities help organisations build remarkable employer brand identities and intelligent online recruitment platforms.

Core offerings include:

- Design and build of bespoke recruitment/careers websites and platforms.
- Development of Employer Brand Identities and EVPs (Employee Value Propositions).
- Design and build of social intranet platforms.
- Recruitment gamification platforms.
- Design and build of bespoke mobile applications.
- Social media advertising and strategy.
- Video production and marketing.
- Online & offline marketing collateral.
- Google Adwords.

CONNECT WITH RICHARD

email
richard@bold-identities.com

linkedin
www.linkedin.com/in/richarde1

twitter
@richevans_

website
www.bold-identities.com

48483473R00097

Made in the USA
Middletown, DE
19 September 2017